M

SELECTED

SU TU

D0096784

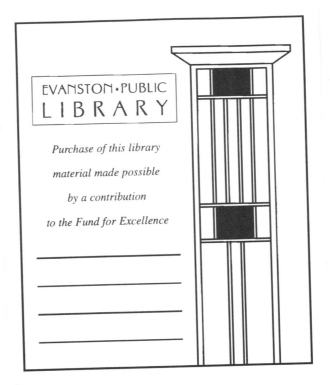

Selected Poems of Su Tung-p'o

TRANSLATED BY

Burton Watson

COPPER CANYON PRESS

Many of these poems originally appeared in *Su Tung-p'o: Selections from a Sung Dynasty Poet*, Columbia University Press, 1965.

Publication of this book is supported by a grant from the National Endowment for the Arts and a grant from the Lannan Foundation. Additional support to Copper Canyon Press has been provided by the Andrew W. Mellon Foundation, the Lila Wallace–Reader's Digest Fund, and the Washington State Arts Commission. Copper Canyon Press is in residence with Centrum at Fort Worden State Park.

Library of Congress Cataloging-in-Publication Data

Su, Shih. 1036-1101.

[Poems. English. Selections]
Selected poems of Su Tung-p'o / translated by Burton Watson.
      p.   cm.
Translated from Chinese.
Expanded version of: Su Tung-p'o.
ISBN 1-55659-064-4
I. Watson, Burton, 1925-. II. Sun Tung-p'o. III. Title.
PL 2685.A6 1994
895.1´142 – DC20   93-28332

THIRD PRINTING

COPPER CANYON PRESS
P.O. BOX 271, PORT TOWNSEND, WA 98368

*For Gary Snyder
and Joanne Kyger*

Contents

SELECTED POEMS OF
SU TUNG-P'O

Introduction

CULTURALLY, the Sung period was one of the great ages of Chinese history. The dynasty, which lasted from 960 to 1279, faced powerful enemies abroad: the Liao, a Khitan state in the northeast; a Tangut state called Hsi-hsia in the northwest; and later the Jurchen Tungus and Mongols. Militarily too weak to overpower these menacing neighbors, it was forced to buy peace with heavy tribute, at the same time maintaining costly border defenses in case of duplicity. Internally this hard-bought peace was put to good use. The empire was ruled by a strong central government whose elaborate bureaucracy functioned, at least until the fiscal strain of national defense became intolerable, with considerable efficiency. Cities grew in size, trade flourished, and education, encouraged by the civil service examination system and spread through government schools and private academies, reached a larger number of people than ever before. New philosophical systems evolved, voluminous histories and encyclopedias were compiled, and painting and porcelain reached their highest level of development.

In comparison with the preceding centuries, the Sung period was also strikingly modern in character. By Sung times the Chinese had gotten up off the floor and were sitting on chairs, contraptions that came in from the west with Buddhism and spread slowly throughout Chinese society; they were reading printed books, drinking tea, carrying on at least part of their monetary transactions with paper money, and experimenting with explosive weapons. Many of them lived in large cities – the main Sung capital, K'ai-feng, was almost certainly the largest city in the world at that time – and traveled freely about the empire by boat, horse, carriage, or palanquin over an elaborate system of roads and waterways. In their way of life, their values, and their interests, the Sung people were in many respects far closer to modern Western life than European men and women of the same period.

This perhaps explains why so much of their poetry reads like the product of our own time. Less intense and less brilliant than that of the T'ang, it is broader in scope and of greater philosophic depth and com-

plexity. Whereas earlier poets had regarded certain themes as intrinsi-
cally outside the pale of poetry, the Sung poets tried their hand at every
subject imaginable, from iron mines to body lice. Where T'ang poets
were content to employ one perfect and profoundly suggestive meta-
phor, Sung poets piled up metaphors until they were satisfied they had
said all they wanted to say – and, as the enormous volume of their
work (estimated at several hundred thousand extant poems) suggests,
they had a great deal to say. Poetry was for the Sung gentleman, even
more than for his predecessor in the T'ang, a part of everyday life, a
normal medium for expressing his thoughts and feelings on any subject
he chose.

The work of Su Shih, the greatest of the Sung poets, more com-
monly known by his literary name, Su Tung-p'o,[1] well illustrates these
qualities. He was born in 1037 in Mei-shan, a town situated at the foot
of Mount O-mei in present-day Szechwan Province.[2] His remote fam-
ily background is uncertain, though there is reason to believe that his
people were connected with the local weaving industry. His grand-
father was illiterate, and his father, Su Hsün, did not begin serious lit-
erary studies until he was in his late twenties, though his father's older
brother passed the civil service examination and became an official. His
mother was from a prominent family, an educated woman and a devout
Buddhist, and undoubtedly had a great influence upon her son's devel-
opment. He had only one brother, Su Ch'e or Su Tzu-yu, three years
younger than himself.

Su Tung-p'o and his brother were educated by their parents and at a
private school in the neighborhood run by a Taoist priest, and by 1056
they felt confident enough to go to K'ai-feng to take the government
civil service examinations. Their father had taken them earlier and

---

1. *Su* is pronounced like *Sue, Shih* like *Sher,* and *Tung-p'o* like *Doong-paw.*

2. He was born on the nineteenth day of the twelfth lunar month of *ching-yu* 3d year,
and since *ching-yu* 3 corresponds largely to A.D. 1036, this is customarily given as his
birth date. But the Chinese year began in February, so that the nineteenth day of the
twelfth month actually fell in early 1037. This is the kind of inconsequential informa-
tion I would ordinarily consider hardly worth reporting; I do so here merely to explain
why my date differs from the customary one.

failed, but he accompanied his sons to the capital. The boys passed the first examination with distinction, and in the following year passed the second, receiving the *chin-shih* degree. At the same time Su Hsün won private recognition of his literary ability from prominent scholars in the capital.

Upon the death of their mother in 1057, the sons returned with their father to Szechwan to observe the customary three year mourning period, actually a period of twenty-seven months. The three journeyed to the capital again in 1060, where Su Hsün received an official appointment and his sons, after passing the special examination the following year, were assigned to posts in the provinces. Thus the so-called Three Sus, father and sons, were launched on the careers that would make their names famous in Chinese literary and political history.

I will not trace here all the moves in the subsequent career of the poet; it would be tedious and confusing, and all the information the reader needs will be supplied later in notes to the poems. Instead I will list the principal facts in outline:

1061-65   Su Tung-p'o served as assistant magistrate in Shensi.
1065   Returned to the capital.
1066   Su Hsün died. His sons accompanied the body home
       to Szechwan and observed the mourning period.
       This was their last trip home.
1068   The two brothers occupied posts in the capital.
1071-79   Out of favor with the ruling clique in the capital, Su
       Tung-p'o moved about in a series of provincial posts.
       In the seventh month of 1079, he was arrested on
       charges of slandering the emperor, imprisoned in the
       capital, released, and banished to Huang-chou.

The last entry demands explanation. The dynasty's administrative and fiscal system was functioning badly because of the heavy strain of tribute and defense expenditures, and most thinking men of the time, including Su Tung-p'o and his father, agreed that reforms were needed. Attempts along this line had been made earlier, and when a forceful new statesman named Wang An-shih (1021-86) came to prominence in

1069, he began, with the full support of the ruler, Emperor Shen-tsung, a vigorous reform program known as the "New Laws." Just what these new laws were need not concern us here, but they were sufficiently radical to offend the more conservative elements in the government and, perhaps more from faulty administration than from the provisions of the laws themselves, caused considerable hardship in the provinces. Su Tung-p'o, living in the provinces, could see the hardship at first hand, and became more and more outspoken in his criticisms, until his enemies in the capital could no longer tolerate him. Using statements in his own poems as evidence, they tried him on charges of slander and effected what amounted to banishment by assigning him an insignificant post in the region of Huang-chou on the north bank of the Yangtze in central China. I would like to note, however, that by this time Wang An-shih, to whom is usually assigned all the blame for the failures and abuses of the reform program, was out of political life and living in retirement at Nanking. However much Su may have disagreed with Wang's political opinions, he seems to have borne no grudge against Wang himself, but on the contrary exchanged poems with him and went out of his way to visit him in later years. Political feelings ran high, but these were highly civilized men. Under the Sung, Su Tung-p'o and those who thought like him suffered the inconvenience and disgrace of banishment. Under almost any earlier dynasty they would very likely have lost their heads.

1080-84 Exiled to Huang-chou.

1085 Returned to the capital and high political office after the overthrow of the "New Laws" party.

1086-93 Held various posts in the capital and the provinces.

1094 Banished a second time with the return of the "New "Laws" party to power. Ordered to proceed to Hui-chou in Kwangtung, east of present-day Canton.

1097 Ordered even farther south to the island of Hainan.

1100 Permitted to return to the mainland; restored to favor and office.

1101 Became ill and died at Ch'ang-chou in Chekiang.

Two facts about the poet's life will be apparent from this outline. One is that he spent all his adult years moving about from place to place, from office to office, which is why so much of his poetry deals with journeys. This was the ordinary life of a Chinese bureaucrat. After a man had entered the administration, usually by way of the civil service examinations, he was assigned to a post, sometimes in the capital but more often in the provinces. In the Sung period it was usual for an official to remain at a particular provincial post no longer than three years — long enough to learn what he needed to know about the region, but not so long that he would begin to identify himself too closely with local interests. Hence a man like Su Tung-p'o was destined to pick up his family and move, say good-by to old friends and start out to make new ones, at least every three years and sometimes oftener. The life of a high provincial official was not particularly difficult, his duties were hardly taxing, and, in normal times at least, his income was sufficient; but he was never permitted to stay in one place long enough to put down roots. Rootless wandering is said to be a characteristic of present-day Americans, but it is hard to think of any group in America, except perhaps migratory laborers, who could match the old-style Chinese official on this score.

Second, if Su Tung-p'o had been inclined toward bitterness, he had plenty of cause for it. Not only was he obliged by the bureaucratic system to spend almost all of his life in separation from his homeland and the one person he felt closest to, his brother Tzu-yu; he was twice forced by political shifts into exile, the second time at an advanced age and to the torrid southernmost extremity of the empire. These periods of banishment not only brought disgrace and the frustration of all his political ambitions, but often involved real physical hardship. The surprising thing is that if he felt bitter or sorry for himself he seldom shows it in his poems. He writes occasionally in a mood of depression or despair; the infrequency of meetings with his brother is a theme that always brings out a strain of sadness. But he seems to have possessed an irrepressible interest in life, an engagement with his fellow human beings and his surroundings that made it impossible for him to brood for long. Far from being bitter, he is actually one of the most cheerful of the great Chinese poets.

He was not only a first-class poet and prose writer, but a distinguished painter and calligrapher as well, and he saw with a painter's eye. His descriptive passages are not limited to the conventional props and landscapes of earlier poetry, but depict all kinds of scene down to the most commonplace; within the confines of Chinese verse form, they are masterpieces of precision and detail. He tells the reader exactly what flowers are blooming, exactly what crops are growing in the fields, just what the weather is like and what people are doing. When later Chinese critics sometimes complained that his poetry lacks suggestiveness, it was probably this very fullness and precision they were objecting to.

He was also, like most major Sung poets, a philosopher. Although he has left no systematic exposition of his ideas, repeatedly he breaks into the descriptive passages of his poems with philosophical meditation. By Sung times, the sea of faith that had been Chinese Buddhism at its height was receding, and native Confucian ways of thought, oriented about the family and the state and strongly rational and humanistic, were beginning to reassert themselves. Su's own philosophy represents a combination of Confucian and Buddhist ideas, with a large mixture of philosophical Taoism.

The Confucian side of his thinking is less apparent in his poetry than in his political papers and his life as a whole – his strong family devotion, the fact that he chose a career in politics, the fearlessness with which he spoke out against abuses in government, the numerous public works for the benefit of the local inhabitants that he undertook at his various provincial posts. In his poetry it is rather the Buddhist and the Taoist aspects of his thinking that find expression. His mother, it will be recalled, was a devout Buddhist. He himself took considerable interest in Buddhist literature and doctrine, and spent much time visiting temples in the areas where he was assigned. After his dismissal from office and banishment to Huang-chou in 1080 this interest deepened; and the influence of Buddhist thought, particularly that of the Ch'an or Zen sect, the most active and intellectual of the Buddhist schools at this time, is apparent in his writings of this period. It was also at this time that he began to call himself Tung-p'o chü-shih or "The Layman of Eastern Slope," after the plot of land he farmed. From this title his literary name of Tung-p'o derives.

The influence of Taoism is most clearly seen in his sensitivity to the natural world. He was fascinated by stories of immortal spirits, elixirs of long life, and other popular lore, and good-naturedly took part in prayers for rain and similar ceremonies of the folk religion, though the rational Confucian side of his nature told him there was no basis for such acts or beliefs. And yet he repeatedly refers to a supernatural force which he calls "The Creator," a word taken from the works of Chuang Tzu, and which he often describes in terms applicable to a child. It is a force which moves throughout the natural world, childlike in its lack of thought or plan, yet capable of influencing the destinies of all beings in the universe. And when human beings learn to be equally free of willfulness and join in the Creator's game, then everything in the natural world will become their toy. It is no accident that Su in his descriptions of nature makes far freer use of personification and pathetic fallacy than any of his predecessors.

Su experimented with nearly every form in traditional Chinese literature. In my selection, three poetic forms are represented (plus an excerpt from one of his letters). Most of the poems I have translated are in the *shih* form, the standard form of classical Chinese poetry, characterized generally by lines of equal length and, with rare exceptions, an even number of lines. Enjambment is rare; there is almost always a pause at the end of each line. Poems in this form fall into two groups: those in the so-called old style, which allows occasional lines of irregular length and does not require any set tonal pattern within the lines; and those in the "modern style," which demands lines of equal length and sometimes of fixed number, and requires an elaborate internal tonal pattern the rules of which are too complex to go into here. Both forms employ end rhyme; sometimes the same rhyme is used throughout a single poem, sometimes in longer poems it changes at points where the poem shifts direction. Su composed in both styles, in most cases using a five-character or seven-character line.

Poetry was part of the everyday social life of an educated man in China, and it was customary for friends and acquaintances to exchange poems on various occasions or to get together and compose poems on a particular theme. Sometimes they assigned rhymes to each other;

sometimes they composed poems employing the same rhyme as that of a friend's poem to which they were responding, occasionally (a real tour de force) using not only the same rhyme, but the very same rhyme words in the same order as those of the original poem. Su mentions all these practices in the introductions to his poems; he even carried the game a step farther by composing poems to the same rhymes as those of a poet of the distant past, T'ao Yüan-ming (365-427).

Nearly all the poems translated here are descriptions of actual occurrences in the poet's life or scenes he had encountered. A few, however, belong to a genre very popular among Chinese poets: that of the poem written to accompany a painting, describing not an actual landscape but a pictured one. Because of their artificial and secondhand nature such poems have seldom appealed to me, but Su, as so often with other forms, has succeeded in giving life even to this rather stilted genre, and I have therefore included several poems of this type.

The second poetic form represented in my selection is the *tz'u*, which employs lines of unequal length but follows a set line, rhyme, and tonal pattern. The *tz'u* were originally songwords written to accompany tunes that came in from Central Asia. It became the custom to write numerous lyrics to fit a single tune, so that in time a number of fixed metrical patterns were established, each known by the name of the tune it fitted. In late T'ang and Five Dynasties times, when the genre was new, these *tz'u* usually dealt with mildly erotic themes and were considered somewhat less respectable than the *shih*, but by Sung times the situation was changing. Su Tung-p'o, one of the acknowledged masters of the *tz'u* form, employed it to treat many of the same themes he treated in his *shih*. He thus opened up new areas of expression for the *tz'u*, though the people of his day, who did not always appreciate this fact, complained that his *tz'u* were actually *shih* in disguise. They also complained that his *tz'u* were difficult to sing, but since the tunes of the *tz'u* were lost long ago, we cannot tell just what they meant by this.

The third poetic form is represented by Su's two famous *fu* or prose poems on the Red Cliff. The *fu* form is old in Chinese literature and before Sung times it was employed usually for lengthy descriptive pieces, often of a fantastic nature, or briefer evocations of emotional states.

It is most often a mixture of prose passages and rhymed sections, the latter in strongly rhythmical patterns with elaborate use of parallelism. Su employs a variation of the form know as *wen fu* or "prose *fu*," which is extremely loose in structure and makes only sparing use of rhyme and parallelism. Even so, it retains a sensuousness of language and rhythmical swing that set it off from pure prose.

Su wrote rapidly and, unlike many of his contemporaries, did not often go back to polish and rewrite.[3] Some 2,400 poems of his have been preserved, about ninety percent of which can be dated. Many of them were printed and published during his lifetime, and though for political reasons his works were banned for a while after his death, the ban was later lifted and his writings circulated freely and widely. They have thus come down to us in excellent condition. Information on texts used in this translation will be found in the Translator's Note that follows.

The Chinese literary tradition, particularly in poetry, grew by feeding upon itself, and it is only natural that Su's poetry should contain echoes of earlier works, phrases and lines which he borrowed from his predecessors and adapted to his own use. Chinese commentators make it their job to point out such borrowings, and a glance at their notes on his poetry is apt to give the impression that his language is unduly

---

3. As an example of the fastidious craftmanship of one of his contemporaries, let me quote a poem by the statesman Wang An-shih, a celebrated poet in his own right. Entitled "Anchoring at Kua-chou," it was probably written in 1075 when Wang, after a brief period of retirement near Nanking, was on his way back to the capital to resume official duties. Ching-k'ou was on the south bank of the Yangtze near Mt. Chung, where Wang's home was; Kua-chou was opposite it, on the north bank.

> Between Ching-k'ou and Kua-chou, one stretch of water;
> Mount Chung right there beyond a few folded hills.
> Spring wind of itself turns the south shore green,
> but what bright moon will light me home?

According to the report of a man who had seen Wang's original manuscript, for the third line he had first written "Again the spring wind reaches the south shore." He crossed out "reaches" (writing in the margin "No good!") and changed it to "passes." This he later changed to "enters," then to "fills," and finally – after also changing "again" to "of itself" – he settled on the word *lu* (to turn green). (Hung Mai, *Jung-chai hsü-pi*, ch. 8.)

bookish and derivative. This is not so. When he wrote, Chinese poetry already had a history of some fifteen hundred years, and he could hardly have avoided repeating the usages of the past without straining for novelty at every turn. A good poet was expected to draw aptly and skillfully upon the works of his predecessors, thereby adding a richness of association to his diction. But a great one had to have such complete mastery of the tradition that he could at the same time express his own thoughts freely and naturally, and could advance and enrich the tradition in some way, adding new depth and nuance. This Su Tung-p'o did. I have appended notes to the translations only where the understanding of an allusion is vital to the understanding of the poem itself, since in any case the echoes of the past which fill the originals must inevitably be lost in translation. It is an indication of Su's greatness, however, that these allusions and associations constitute only a minor part of the interest of his poetry, and that without any knowledge of them his works can still be read with enjoyment and profit.

My selection consists of 112 poems, plus the two prose poems and the excerpt from a letter mentioned above, which I have arranged in chronological order and divided into five parts for the sake of convenience. I have naturally chosen poems which I like and which I think go well into English. At the same time, I have tried to suggest the breadth of forms used and subjects treated by the poet, and to convey something of his distinctive personality. Some of his poems have titles, but others are prefaced only by introductory remarks; I have therefore used the first line as a title where Su has not supplied one. My hardest task has been to limit the size of the selection. Faced with so many poems, prose writings, and letters, of such intrinsic merit and interest, a translator has to exercise rigid control if his work is ever to reach a stopping point.

Translator's Note

LIKE my volume of translations from Han-shan (*Cold Mountain*, New York, Grove Press, 1962), this book is based upon the work of a Japanese scholar: two volumes of translations from Su Tung-p'o, by Ogawa Tamaki, Professor of Chinese Literature at Kyoto University, entitled *So Shoku*, published in 1962. These comprise numbers 5 and 6 in the second series of the *Chūgoku shijin senshū* (Selected works of Chinese poets) published by Iwanami Shoten, Tokyo. I have made my own selection, omitting many of the poems in Ogawa's selection and including others that he does not include; but his work provided the foundation for mine, and he has been kind enough to go over with me the pieces I have added. I am deeply grateful for the time and assistance he has given me. I am also indebted to other volumes in the same series for material in the introduction and notes, particularly the *Sōshi gaisetsu* (Introduction to Sung poetry) by Professor Yoshikawa Kojiro (no. 1, 2d series, 1962) and *Ō Anseki* (Wang An-shih) by Professor Shimizu Shigeru (no. 4, 2d series, 1962).

For readers interested in the life of Su Tung-p'o, there is a full-length biography in English by Lin Yutang entitled *The Gay Genius* (New York, John Day, 1947). Lin's treatment of political issues is fiercely partisan, and for some reason he records lunar calendar dates in solar calendar terms without making any conversion, so that all his day and month dates are a month or so too early. But his work contains a tremendous amount of detailed information on the poet's life and times, as well as a number of translations of his poetry. There are two volumes of English translations from the *fu* or prose poems of Su Tung-p'o by C.D. Le Gros Clark: *Selections from Su Tung P'o* (London, Jonathan Cape, Ltd., 1931), and *The Prose Poetry of Su Tung P'o* (Shanghai, 1935); these contain valuable introductory material on the poet and his work. Translations of 25 of Su's poems are included in Kenneth Rexroth's *One Hundred Poems from the Chinese* (Norfolk, Conn., New Directions, 1956); anonymous translations of 34 poems, both *shih* and *tz'u*, appeared in *Chinese Literature* (Peking), 1962, no. 12, pp. 59-80.

My own work is put forward not as a literary biography or a study of the poet and his works, but simply as a selection of poems in translation. Chronological order provides a convenient framework, and I hope that the biographical notes I have supplied from time to time will increase the reader's understanding of the poems. But I would ask that the translations themselves be regarded as the heart of the book. I have deliberately kept introductory matter to a minimum, partly because I am very much an amateur in the study of Sung history and culture, and also because I do not believe that a great deal of background and exegesis is necessary for an appreciation of the poems. Readers who wish further information on the poetry of Su Tung-p'o and Sung poetry in general are referred to the works mentioned above and to my translation of Professor Yoshikawa's *Sōshi gaisetsu: An Introduction to Sung Poetry* (Cambridge, Mass.: Harvard University Press, 1967).

Detailed information on the numerous Chinese and Japanese editions and commentaries on Su's writings will be found in Lin, pp. 399–413, and Ogawa, I, 18–21. Editions by Ch'ing scholars, notably the exhaustive work by Wang Wen-kao published in 1822 and reprinted in 1888 (*Su Wen-chung-kung-shih pien-chu chi-ch'eng*), which arrange the poems in chronological order, are invaluable for an understanding of the poet's life and literary growth. Since I have followed chronological order in my arrangement, the reader should have no trouble locating the originals in such an edition.

Part One

EARLY YEARS: 1059 TO 1073

On the Yangtze Watching the Hills (1059)

1   From the boat watching hills — swift horses:
a hundred herds race by in a flash.
Ragged peaks before us suddenly change shape,
ranges behind us start and rush away.
I look up: a narrow trail angles back and forth,
a man walking it, high in the distance.
I wave from the deck, trying to call,
but the sail takes us south like a soaring bird.

Husband-Watching Height (1059)

LEGEND says that long ago a woman whose husband had gone down river to Ch'u used to climb to the height overlooking the Yangtze to watch for his return, until in time she turned to stone.

2   Single stone on the mountaintop,
          looming in the distance,
     where the river bends and boats turn,
          stone like a screen —
     pitiful, a thousand years ago,
          it might be yesterday,
     and the boats come, the boats go,
          never ever stopping.
     Vast, unbroken, the long river
          rolls on to the gray sea;
     in endless lines, travelers pass
          like duckweed drifting by.
     Who'll sit and wait with me
          till the mountain moon comes up?
     By its light we'll see that cold form
          towering lonely and forlorn.

Spring Night

3 Spring night – one hour worth a thousand gold coins;
clear scent of flowers, shadowy moon.
Songs and flutes upstairs – threads of sound;
in the garden, a swing, where night is deep and still.

Traveling at Night and Looking at the Stars (1060)

4 Heaven high above, the night air chill,
ranged stars crowd the sky, all in proper places,
big stars darting rays back and forth,
little stars busy as boiling water.
Heaven and humans don't meddle with one another –
what does Heaven do anyway? –
but it's our habit to insist on pointing at things
and one by one assigning them names.
Southern Sieve, Northern Dipper –
what are these but household utensils?
What would Heaven do with their like?
We're the ones who decided to call them that.
Peer at things up close and you may learn their true form,
but guessed at from afar, they seem like something else.
Vastness such as this is beyond comprehension –
all I can do is sigh in endless wonder.

Hsin-ch'ou Eleventh Month, Nineteenth Day (1061)

HSIN-CH'OU eleventh month, nineteenth day: having parted from
Tzu-yu outside the Cheng-chou west gate, I wrote this poem on
horseback and sent it to him.

5 I haven't been drinking – why this wobbly drunken feeling?
My heart races after you as you turn your horse toward home,
the homebound thinking of course of a parent there,
but how am I to ease my loneliness?
Climbing a rise, I look back – you've gone beyond the slope;
all I see is a black hat bobbing up, then disappearing.
Bitter cold, and I recall what thin clothes you're wearing,
riding alone on a skinny horse, treading the last of the moonlight.
People go down the road singing, people in houses are merry;
my groom can't understand why I'm so terribly downcast.
Even *I* know life must have its partings;
I'm just afraid the months and years will whirl away too soon!
Facing each other by the cold lamp – I remember it as yesterday.
When will we listen to the soft rustle of night rain?
You too know these things mustn't be forgotten.
Careful – don't get too wrapped up in dreams of high office!

Rhyming with Tzu-yu's "At Mien-ch'ih, Recalling the Past" (1061)

6 Wanderings of a lifetime – what do they resemble?
  A winging swan that touches down on snow-soaked mud.
  In the mud by chance he leaves the print of his webs,
  but the swan flies away, who knows to east or west?
  The old monk is dead now, become a new memorial tower;
  on the crumbling wall, impossible to find our old inscriptions.
  Do you recall that day, steep winding slopes,
  road long, all of us tired, our lame donkeys braying?

Line 8. A note by the poet explains that they were riding donkeys because their horses had died midway in the journey.

Song of the Stone Drums (1061)

7 Winter, twelfth month, the year *hsin-ch'ou* (1061),
   I first took government office, called on the old man of Lu.
   From times past I'd heard of the stone drums, now I saw them,
   their dense fearful characters like slithering snakes or dragons.
   Peering closer, I started trying to write the words on my stomach,
   longing to read them, but alas! my mouth was fettered.
   Han Yü loved antiquity, but even he lived too late,
   and what of me, born a hundred years after!
   I strained to make out the radicals, guessing at the rest,
   sometimes getting a word or two, missing eight or nine:
   "Our chariots are stalwart, our horses well paired…"
   "For fish he has tench strung on willow wands…"
   as though in an array of antique vessels I recognized only a cauldron,
   or in the jumbled maze of stars could barely name the Dipper.
   All was muddled, hazy, half-hidden in nicks and scars,
   tangled convolutions, here and there a heel or elbow.
   Or like a lovely crescent moon wreathed in clouds and mist,
   sleek stalks of auspicious grain soaring above weeds and stubble.
   Washed over by a hundred battles, you yet managed to survive;
   standing alone a thousand years, who befriended you?
   Your inscriptions would have drawn approval from Ts'ang Chieh
      of high antiquity;
   Ping and Ssu of later ages were mere fledglings to you.
   I think of long ago, King Hsüan, the "Wild Geese" song;
   at that time his scribe Chou reformed the tadpole characters.
   Weary of chaos, men longed for sage rulers, worthy ministers;
   to restore the dynasty, Heaven brought forth those old men.
   Fierce as snarling tigers they struck east at the Hsü barbarians;
   north they subdued the Dog Jung, teaching them to heel.
   Tribes flocked to our interpreters, wolves and deer their tribute;
   Fang and Shao repeatedly received jade batons and wine vessels in
      reward.

So when the war drums sounded, men looked to their commanders;
no need then for the percussions of the court's blind musicians.
Who composed the hymns incised here, equal to "Mount Sung
    Lofty"?
Forever they'll rank beside the Kou-lou inscription.
Superb were the deeds accomplished, yet there's no boasting;
the age of Wen and Wu not far away, truthfulness prevailed.
I try to date the stones but they've no cyclical signs,
much less a name to show who fashioned them.
In the twilight of Chou's power, the Seven States appeared,
then at last the men of Ch'in took possession of the Nine Provinces.
They snatched away the *Odes* and *Documents*, intoning laws instead;
cast aside the implements of sacrifice, replaced them with whips and
    manacles.
Who at that time aided the Primal Dragon?
A gentleman of Shang-ts'ai leading his yellow dog.
The ruler, ascending mountains, had stones inscribed to laud his
    achievements,
deeds unmatched in later ages, without rival in the past.
All told how the August Emperor toured the lands in four directions,
"wiping out the powerful and unruly, rescuing the black-headed
    people."
The Six Confucian Classics reduced to dust and ashes,
these stone drums too must have faced destruction.
Hearing that the Nine Cauldrons were sunk in the Ssu River,
the ruler had ten thousand men dive under the water to retrieve
    them.
In his willfulness the tyrant wore out men's strength,
but the holy objects, righteous, would not be sullied by Ch'in's filth.
At that time where did the stone drums hide?
Surely Heaven must have commanded the spirits to guard them.
Rise and fall, a hundred shifts, but these objects remain serene;
wealth, honor – gone in a morning! Only names endure.
I ponder the principle behind it all, sigh in spite of myself.
How can we humans gain longevity like yours?

THE DRUMS, ten large drum-shaped stones with carved inscriptions on nine of them, were discovered in the T'ang. Scholars, highly excited by the find, labored to decipher the inscriptions and wrote poems on the subject, the most famous being "Song of the Stone Drums" by Han Yü (768–824). This poem by Su is accordingly often referred to as "The Later Song of the Stone Drums." In Su's time the drums were thought to date from the reign of King Hsüan (r. 827–782) of the Chou, though they are now believed to have been produced in the state of Ch'in in the time of Duke Hsiang (777–766) or of Duke Ling (424–415). By Su's time they had been moved from their original site to the Confucian temple at Feng-hsiang. They are now preserved in Peking.

Line 2. On assuming office, Su went first to the Confucian temple in Feng-hsiang to pay his respects to Confucius, a native of Lu.

Line 24. Ts'ang Chieh is the mythic inventor of the Chinese writing system in the time of the Yellow Emperor. Ping is Li Yang-ping, a famous calligrapher of T'ang times. Ssu is Li Ssu (d. 208 B.C.), Ch'in dynasty statesman and reformer of the writing system, likewise renowned for his calligraphy.

Line 28. King Hsüan restored order to the empire after a time of troubles and revived the fortunes of the Chou dynasty. The song "Wild Geese" in the *Book of Odes* (#181) was believed to extol his reign. His scribe Chou invented a new style of writing, the Large Seal characters, to replace the tadpole-shaped characters of high antiquity.

Line 32. Fang Shu and Shao Hu were military leaders in the time of King Hsüan. These lines draw on events and persons mentioned in the *Book of Odes*.

Line 36. "Mount Sung Lofty," #259 in the *Book of Odes*, celebrates famous men of the time of King Hsüan. The Kou-lou stone inscription was believed to date from the time of the legendary sage ruler Yü. It stood on the Kou-lou peak of Mount Heng in Hunan.

Line 38. Kings Wen and Wu founded the Chou dynasty, probably around 1045 B.C. King Hsüan was the eleventh ruler of the dynasty.

Line 44. The state of Ch'in, one of the Seven States of the Warring States period (403–221), conquered its rivals and united the empire (the Nine Provinces) under a single rule, in 221 B.C. founding a new dynasty. The First Emperor of the Ch'in ordered the burning of the Confucian Classics, which included the *Book of Odes* and *Book of Documents*, and instead supported the teachings of the Legalist School of philosophy, which called for strict regimentation of the populace.

Line 46. The Primal Dragon refers to the First Emperor; in the year of his death a mysterious figure appeared and announced, "This year the Primal Dragon will die!" The gentleman of Shang-ts'ai is Li Ssu, famous prime minister of Ch'in who helped the First Emperor carry out his harsh measures. Ousted from power by a rival and condemned to death, he said to his son as they faced execution, "I wish you and I could once more take our yellow dog and go out the eastern gate of Shang-ts'ai to chase the wily rabbits. But there's little hope of that, is there!"

Line 50. Quoted from the inscription recording the First Emperor's ascent of Mount Chih-fu in 218 B.C.

Line 54. The Nine Cauldrons were ancient symbols of power, supposedly cast in the time of the sage ruler Yü. They were believed to have sunk into the Ssu River in the closing years of the Chou. The First Emperor's attempt to recover them took place in 219 B.C. and ended in failure.

The Statue of Vimalakirti, a Clay Figure by Yang Hui-chih of the T'ang in the Temple of the Pillar of Heaven (1061)

8 Long ago when Master Yü was sick and dying,
his friend Master Ssu went to visit him.
Stumbling to the well, Yü looked in and sighed,
"What will the Creator make out of me next?"
Now as I view this old clay image of Vimalakirti,
ailing bones sharp and knobby, like a dried-up turtle,
I know that a great man is indifferent to life and death,
his body changing form, gone with the floating clouds.
Most people – yes, they're sturdy and handsome,
but though not sick in body, their minds are worn out.
This old fellow – his spirit's whole, something solid inside;
with quip and laughter he overpowers a thousand contenders.
When he was alive someone asked him about the Dharma;
he bowed his head, wordless, though at heart of course he knew.
To this day his likeness sits stolid, never speaking,
just as he was in life, nothing added, nothing lost.
Old farmers, village wives never deign to give a glance,
though field mice sometimes nibble at his whiskers.
Each time I look at him I'm lost in wonder –
Who can be like Vimalakirti, a wordless teacher?

VIMALAKIRTI was a wealthy lay follower of Shakyamuni Buddha in India, famous for his masterful understanding of the Buddha's teachings and his skill in propounding them. He is the central figure in the *Vimalakirti Sutra*, one of the most important texts of Mahayana Buddhism. Yang Hui-chih was a painter and sculptor active in the early eighth century. The T'ien-chu-ssu or Temple of the Pillar of Heaven was in Feng-hsiang.

Lines 1-4. These lines are based on the passage in *Chuang Tzu* Sec. 6 that describes Master Yü's calm acceptance of death and tells how, dragging himself haltingly to the well and looking in, he speculated on what form the Creator intended him to take next.

Line 8. As a means of teaching the truths of Buddhism, Vimalakirti took on the form of an ailing man. In the *Vimalakirti Sutra* ch. 2 he says: "This body is like a floating cloud, changing and fading away in an instant."

Line 14. *Vimalakirti Sutra* ch. 9 describes how the bodhisattva Manjushri asked Vimalakirti to give his interpretation of nondualism, the core concept of the Dharma or Buddhist doctrine. Vimalakirti replied by remaining silent.

Seeing the Year Out (1062)

THREE POEMS on the year's end. At the end of the year, we call on each other with gifts of food, and this custom is known as "Year End Presents." We drink and eat together and exchange greetings, and this is called "Saying Goodby to the Old Year." Then on the last night we stay up until dawn, and this is known as "Seeing the Year Out." This is the custom in Shu. Now I am assigned to a post at Mount Ch'i [Feng-hsiang], and when the end of the year came, I thought of how it would be to return to Shu. But of course it was impossible, so I wrote these three poems to send to Tzu-yu.

9 Want to know what the passing year is like?
A snake slithering down a hole.
Half his long scales already hidden,
how to stop him from getting away?
Grab his tail and pull, you say?
Pull all you like – it does no good.
The children try hard not to doze,
chatter back and forth to stay awake,
but I say let dawn cocks keep still!
I fear the noise of watch drums pounding.
We've sat so long the lamp's burned out.
I get up and look at the slanting Dipper.
How could I hope next year won't come?
My mind shrinks from the failures it may bring.
I work to hold on to the night
while I can still brag I'm young.

THIS IS the third of the three poems. Shu is the old name for Szechwan, the region where the poet and his brother were born and reared. It should be remembered that, according to Chinese custom, everyone considers himself a year older with the coming of the New Year.

Rhyming with Tzu-yu's "Treading the Green" (1063)

10   East wind stirs fine dust on the roads:
first chance for strollers to enjoy the new spring.
Slack season – just right for roadside drinking,
grain still too short to be crushed by carriage wheels.
City people sick of walls around them
clatter out at dawn and leave the whole town empty.
Songs and drums jar the hills, grass and trees shake;
picnic baskets strew the fields where crows pick them over.
Who draws a crowd there? A priest, he says,
blocking the way, selling charms and scowling:
"Good for silkworms – give you cocoons like water jugs!
Good for livestock – make your sheep big as deer!"
Passers-by aren't sure they believe his words –
buy charms anyway to consecrate the spring.
The priest grabs their money, heads for a wine shop;
dead drunk, he mutters: "My charms really work!"

WRITTEN while the poet was an official in Feng-hsiang in Shensi. "Treading the Green" refers to a day of picnics and outings traditionally held in early spring.

Line 9. "A priest." *Tao-jen,* a term used for both Buddhist and Taoist priests.

Rhyming with Tzu-yu's "Silkworm Fair" (1063)

11 Shu men work hard for food and clothing;
    Shu men on vacation never want to stop.
    A thousand plow and plant, ten thousand eat;
    one year's sweat and ache, one spring lull.
    In slack time they hold the silkworm fair,
    forget troubles in the scramble for fun.
    Last year at first frost they cut autumn reeds;
    this year silkworm frames are stacked in hills.
    They slice gourds for spindles, mold clay pots;
    fine silk and goldwork aren't all that draw a crowd.
    I remember long ago when you and I were boys;
    each year we dropped our books and raced to the fair.
    Peddlers outdid each other hawking goods;
    peasants stood gaping, ripe to be cheated –
    when your poem came it brought back those times again.
    I grieve less for home than for the years that are lost.

Line 9. "Clay pots." For boiling the cocoons.

It Snowed in South Valley (1063)

TWELFTH MONTH, fourteenth day. Light snow during the night. Next morning early I set out for the village of South Valley, stopped for a bite and a drink on the way, and reached there by evening.

12 It snowed in South Valley — a priceless sight.
I raced my horse to get there before it could melt,
pushing back branches, following the trail alone,
ahead of dawn, first to cross the ocher bridge —
to find roofs caved in, nowhere to spend the night,
villagers starving: their listless voices show it.
Only the twilight crow knows how I feel —
he flies up and the cold limb sheds a thousand flakes.

Following the Rhymes of Yang Pao's "Early Spring" (1070)

13   Slum alleys are still bitter with winter cold,
     but the gardens at your house have turned to spring.
     I don't mind riding a lean horse, shuffling through snow.
     I've come to hear your fine ladies sing "The Nut Tree."
     To break up gloom, brew's the thing to call for;
     we grow old, but who goes on grumbling at the gods?
     Good days, happy times, never come in pairs;
     with white hair and blue coat, I too can sing.
     Fine rain on country fields – shall I plant greens?
     Gate of a poor official – I could stretch a net.
     Our gracious sovereign has given us three days off from court.
     I sleep late mornings and wake up wondering where I am.

Line 8. "Blue coat." The uniform of a low-ranking official. The poet was only thirty-four and could hardly have been very white-headed, but Chinese poets customarily begin complaining of their gray hairs at a very early age.

Line 10. "Stretch a net." From the story of a once-powerful official who, after he lost his position, complained that he had so few visitors he could have stretched a sparrow net across his gate without fear of anyone's stumbling into it. (*Shih chi* 120.)

For Fu Yao-yü's Grass Hall at Chi-yüan (1071)

14 Petty officials all long for the fields,
    but we put off till we're old looking for a country place.
    Seedling to shade tree is a ten year's wait;
    rush to buy land and gold counts for nothing.
    You chose a site by the clear Chi;
    your great trees by now look like groves in a picture.
    Neighbors know how you love bamboo –
    they're careful in spring not to bruise the young shoots.

I Travel Day and Night (1071)

PASSED the place where the Ying River enters the Huai, and for the first time saw the mountains along the Huai. Today we reached Shou-chou.

15   I travel day and night toward the Yangtze and the sea.
Maple leaves, reed flowers – fall has endless sights.
On the broad Huai I can't tell if the sky is near or far;
green hills keep rising and falling with the boat.
Shou-chou – already I see the white stone pagoda
though short oars haven't brought us round Yellow Grass Hill.
Waves calm, wind mild – I look for the landing.
My friends have stood a long time in twilight mist.

Visiting Gold Mountain Temple (1071)

16 My home is where the river first bubbles from a fountain;
now official travels take me to where it meets the sea.
I've heard the tidal bore here rises one *chang* high;
in these cold days its marks still show in the sand.
On the south bank at Chung-leng are the Meditation Rocks,
from times past appearing and disappearing with the waves.
I tried climbing the hilltop, gazing far off at home;
north of the river, south of the river, so many hills!
Travel-worn, wary of nightfall, I asked about boats to the shore,
but mountain monks pressed me to stay and watch the sunset.
Faint wind: on the broad water, wrinkles like creases in a shoe;
ragged clouds: over half the sky, a red the color of fish tails.
Tonight the river moon was a new crescent;
at second watch it set, the sky turning inky black.
In the heart of the river was something bright as a torch,
streaming rays lighting the hills, startling the roosting crows.
I went back to bed puzzled, uncertain what I'd seen –
not human, not ghostly, what could it have been?
All these river hills, and I don't go home to hills of my own –
the river god sent this wonder to chide my stupidity!
Apologies to the river god, but right now what can I do?
If in the end I don't return to homeland fields, let him punish me
    as he will!

Line 3. The bore was at its highest in the eighth lunar month. One *chang* is equal to about twelve feet.

Winter Solstice (1071)

I TOOK an outing to Lone Hill and visited two Buddhist priests, Hui-ch'in and Hui-ssu.

17 The sky threatens snow,
    clouds cover the lake;
    towers appear and disappear, hills loom and fade.
    Clear water cut by rocks – you can count the fish;
    deep woods deserted – birds call back and forth.
    Winter solstice: I refuse to go home to my family;
    I say I'm visiting priests, though really out for fun.
    These priests I visit – where do they live?
    The road by Jewel Cloud Mountain twists and turns.
    Lone Hill's alone indeed – who'd live here?
    These priests – the hill's not lonely after all.
    Paper windows, bamboo roof – rooms sheltered and warm;
    in coarse robes they doze on round rush mats.
    Cold day, a long road – my servant grumbles,
    brings the carriage, hurries me home before dark.
    Down the hill, looking back, clouds and trees blend;
    I can just make out a mountain eagle circling the pagoda.
    Such trips – simple but with a joy that lasts;
    back home, I'm lost in a dreamer's daze.
    Write a poem quick before it gets away!
    Once gone, a lovely sight is hard to catch again.

New Year's Eve (1071)

18 New Year's Eve – you'd think I could go home early
but official business keeps me.
I hold the brush and face them with tears:
Pitiful convicts in chains,
little men who tried to fill their bellies,
fell into the law's net, don't understand disgrace.
And I? In love with a meager stipend
I hold on to my job and miss the chance to retire.
Don't ask who is foolish or wise;
all of us alike scheme for a meal.
The ancients would have freed them a while at New Year's –
would I dare to do likewise? I am silent with shame.

No title. Written in Hangchow. In 1090, when Su wrote another poem on the same rhyme, he described the circumstances under which he wrote this poem. "New Year's Eve I was on duty in the city office, which was full of prisoners in chains. Evening came and still I could not get away and return to my quarters, and so I wrote a poem on the wall." By custom, cases involving the death penalty had to be settled before the New Year, and it was such cases that kept the poet at his office.

The Longevity Joy Hall of the Chung-she Chang of Yüeh-chou (1072)

19 The green hills sprawl like a drowsy hermit
who most times won't go near a government office.
But this "hermit" has a special way with hills –
not waiting to be invited, they crowd his courtyard.
Sleeping Dragon Mountain coils over half of eastern Yüeh,
ten thousand houses like scales encrusting its flank.
If you turn your back so you can't see it, it might as well not exist –
as stupid as wearing a fox fur jacket inside out!
But Mr. Chang has eyes to spy out Nature's secrets;
this thorny waste somehow he's transformed into a home.
Chin in hand he sits at ease, not going out his gate,
raking in half of all the wonderful sights around.
Many talents, little to do, he wearies of so much leisure,
lying and watching clouds and mist turn to wind and rain,
his bamboo shoots like jade chopsticks, mulberries like hairpin
     baubles;
at rare times when he drinks, he plays host to the hills.
He doesn't care if his children know he delights in such things,
only fears the Creator may punish him for having too much.
Late in spring, long nap over, afternoon windows still bright –
I see him now, his bowl of new tea frothing with bubbles!

CHANG TZ'U-SHAN, who held the post of Chung-she or secretary of the heir apparent and whose home is the subject of the poem, was an official of the central government who, clashing with Wang An-shih, was transferred to a provincial post in Yüeh-chou, in present day Shao-hsing in Chekiang.

Viewing Peonies at the Temple of Good Fortune (1072)

20 I'm not ashamed at my age to stick a flower in my hair.
The flower is the embarrassed one, topping an old man's head.
People laugh as I go home drunk, leaning on friends —
ten miles of elegant blinds raised halfway for watching.

In the Rain, Visiting the Temple of the Compassionate Goddess of Mercy (1072)

21   Silkworms grow old, wheat is half yellow;
     on hills ahead, hills behind, rain sluices down.
     Farmers must leave their plows, mulberry girls their baskets;
     the white-robed goddess keeps to her high hall.

Black Clouds – Spilled Ink (1072)

SIXTH MONTH, twenty-seventh day. Drunk at Lake Watch Tower, wrote five poems.

22   Black clouds – spilled ink half blotting out the hills;
pale rain – bouncing beads that splatter in the boat.
Land-rolling wind comes, blasts and scatters them:
below Lake Watch Tower, water like sky.

Evening View from Sea Watch Tower (1072)

23   Where green hills break, story on story of tower;
houses on the other bank – if you called, I think they'd answer!
Autumn wind on the river, by evening blowing stronger,
carrying our bell and drum sounds all the way to Hsi-hsing.

I Only Hear a Bell Beyond the Mist (1072)

READING the little poem written by the priest Shou-ch'üan of the Fan-t'ien Temple, I was so taken by its elegance that I wrote this using the same rhyme.

24   I only hear a bell beyond the mist,
     can't see the mist-wrapped temple.
     The man secluded there never stops walking —
     dew from the grass soaks his straw sandals —
     nothing but the mountaintop moon
     each night to light his comings and goings.

Grasses Bury the River Bank (1072)

SPENT the night at Shui-lu Temple; sent two poems to the priest Ch'ing-shun of North Mountain.

25   Grasses bury the river bank, rain darkens the village;
the temple is lost in tall bamboo – I can't find the gate.
They're gathering wood and brewing herbs – I'm sorry a monk is
    sick;
they've swept the ground and burned incense – it cleans my spirit.
Farm work not finished, though we're into Little Snow;
lamps lit before the Buddha, signal of dusk –
lately I've developed a taste for the quiet life.
I think how we could lie and talk together through the night.

Line 5. "Little Snow." The tenth lunar month, beginning around November 23.

Lament of the Farm Wife of Wu (1072)

26 Rice this year ripens so late!
We watch, but when will frost winds come?
They come – with rain in bucketfuls;
the harrow sprouts mold, the sickle rusts.
My tears are all cried out, but rain never ends;
it hurts to see yellow stalks flattened in the mud.
We camped in a grass shelter a month by the fields;
then it cleared and we reaped the grain, followed the wagon home,
sweaty, shoulders sore, carting it to town –
the price it fetched, you'd think we came with chaff.
We sold the ox to pay taxes, broke up the roof for kindling;
we'll get by for a time, but what of next year's hunger?
Officials demand cash now – they won't take grain;
the long northwest border tempts invaders.
Wise men fill the court – why do things get worse?
I'd be better off bride to the River Lord!

Line 16. "Bride to the River Lord." In ancient times it was the custom each year to sacrifice a young girl as a "bride" to the River Lord, the god of the Yellow River, by placing her on a bed and letting her float down the river until the bed capsized and she drowned.

The Fa-hui Temple's Pavilion of Horizontal Green (1073)

27 Mornings we see Wu hill horizontal,
    evenings we see it rise straight up.
    Wu hill strikes many different poses,
    turning this way and that, showing off for us.
    A man of retiring ways built this red pavilion,
    completely empty, nothing inside,
    only those thousand-pace slopes
    east and west as ornaments to top its blinds.
    Spring comes, but I've no prospect of returning to my homeland;
    they talk of autumn sadness, but spring's even sadder.
    I went boating on the broad lake, thought of Washing Brocade River;
    now I look at horizontal green hills and recall Mount O-mei.
    These carved railings – how long will they keep their beauty?
    The man leaning on them's not the only one to grow suddenly old.
    Ups and downs of a hundred years even sadder to contemplate –
    I see a time when rank grass will bury this pond and tower.
    Then if the traveler should look for spots where I once strolled,
    let his search take him here to the horizontal hills of Wu.

Lines 11-12. Washing Brocade River was a name for the section of the Yangtze near Ch'eng-tu in the area of Su's home; O-mei is close to where he was born.

Wild Birds on the Roof Call Insistently (1073)

28 FIRST MONTH, twenty-first day. Recovered from illness. Shu-ku came to get me and we went outside the city to look at spring.

Wild birds on the roof call insistently;
by the railing, the frozen pond breaks into ripples.
Getting drunk, chasing red skirts — at my age it palls;
up after illness, I wonder at the new gray hairs.
In bed, I heard the governor's drum and bugle,
called the boy to fix my headband and hat.
Winding walks, hidden arbor — how cramped and dull!
Now a look at country meadows, the wide open spring!

HANGCHOW. Ch'en Shu-ku (Ch'en Hsiang) was a high official who, like the poet, failed to get along with the leaders of the reform party and in 1072 was appointed governor of Hangchow.

Drinking at the Lake; It Was Clear at First but Later It Rained. Two Poems (1073)

I.

29 Morning sunlight greets the guests, emblazoning the tiered slopes;
evening rain detains them, escorting them to the land of drunkenness.
Gentlemen, can you appreciate the felicity of these intentions?
Let us offer a cup in tribute to the King of Water Immortals!

II.

30 The gleam of this bright expanse of water, fine while the weather's
  clear;
the color of the hills under a drizzly sky – rain too is superb!
Shall I compare West Lake to the lovely Hsi-tzu,
in light make-up or heavy, equally fine?

30, line 4. Hsi-tzu was a famous beauty of the Hangchow area in ancient times.

On the Road to Hsin-ch'eng (1073)

31   The east wind, knowing I plan to walk through the hills,
hushed the sound of endless rain between the eaves.
On peaks, fair-weather clouds – cloth caps pulled down;
early sun in treetops – a copper gong suspended.
Wild peach smiles over low bamboo hedges;
by clear sandy streams, valley willows sway.
These west hill families must be happiest of all,
boiling cress and roasting shoots to feed spring planters.

Mountain Village (1073)

32   Old man of seventy, sickle at his waist:
      thank God for spring hills – their sprouts and ferns are sweet.
      Is it Shao music's made me forget how things should taste?
      For three months now no salt for my food!

33   With goosefoot staff, boiled rice for the road, he hurries off;
      copper coins in no time will be lost to other hands.
      What's left to show? My son speaks fancy language –
      over half the year we spend in town!

THE THIRD AND FOURTH of five poems written during the trip described in the preceding poem. Both are veiled attacks on Wang An-shih's administration, as the poet admitted later when he was called up for investigation. The first refers to the fact that Wang's tightening of restrictions on the government salt monopoly had made salt all but impossible for the common people to obtain. The second is a jibe at Wang's system of farm loans, which was intended to ease the lot of the farmers by lending them money in the spring and requiring repayment in the fall. To receive and repay the loans, however, the farmers were obliged to make frequent and prolonged trips into town, where the government offices were situated. The poem pictures a farmer setting off on such a trip.

Line 3. "Shao music." According to Analects VII, 13, Confucius, after hearing the ancient Shao music, was so struck with admiration that for three months he forgot the taste of meat.

Visiting the Monastery of the Patriarch's Pagoda While Ill (1073)

34 Purple plums, yellow melons – the village roads smell sweet;
black gauze cap, white hemp robe – traveling clothes are cool.
In a country temple, gate closed, pine shadows turning,
I prop pillows by a breezy window and dream long dreams.
A vacation due to illness – things could be worse;
stilling the mind – no medicine is better than this.
The priests aren't stingy with their well by the stairs;
they gave me pail and dipper and said help yourself!

Roadside Flowers, Three Poems with Introduction (1073)

ON A TRIP to the Mountain of the Nine Immortals [in Lin-an] I heard the village boys singing "Roadside Flowers." The old men told me that the consort of the king of Wu-Yüeh each year in spring would always return to her old home in Lin-an. Then the king would write her a letter saying, "Roadside flowers are in bloom – no hurry, but come on home!" The people of Wu took his words and used them to make a song that is tuneful and full of feeling. When I heard it I found it very moving. But the lyrics were too countrified and so I've written new ones.

I.

35 Roadside flowers are blooming, butterflies on the wing;
rivers and hills remain, but not the people of time gone by.
Subjects of a lost ruler, growing older year by year,
as strolling women keep singing, "No hurry, but come on home!"

II.

36 Wild roadside flowers, blooming in boundless numbers;
along the road people vie to see her curtained carriage go by.
If only there were some way to halt spring's heedless passing –
later on, no hurry, she can go on home.

III.

37 Wealth and honor in life were dew on the grass leaf;
now he's gone, they remember him in "Roadside Flowers."
Slow, slow his steps when the ruler left his kingdom,
and still they tell his wife, "No hurry, but come back home."

Lodging at Hai-hui Temple (1073)

38   Three days by palanquin traveling through mountains;
beautiful mountains, but never a level stretch!
Dip toward the yellow springs, rise to the sky,
contest a thread-thin path with monkeys,
Till we reach a narrow hollow, pagoda tall and cramped in it;
thighs ache with bruises, empty stomach growls.
North across a high bridge, bearers' feet clomping;
walls like old battlements wind a hundred yards.
They sound the great bell — a crowd of monks appears,
leads me to the main hall, unbarred even at night.
Cedar tub and lacquer pail pour out rivers
to wash the body "spotless from the first."
I fall in bed and startle my neighbors with snoring;
the fifth-watch drum booms, the sky still dark.
Sharp and clear the wooden fish calls us to gruel;
I hear no voices, but the scuff of shoes.

Line 3. "Yellow springs." A term for the underworld; Su uses it here facetiously.

Line 12. "Spotless from the first." A Zen term derived from the Vimalakirti Sutra, Sec. 8, referring to the purity of the original nature.

Line 15. "Wooden fish." A board shaped like a fish which was struck to summon the monks to meals.

Written for Master Chan's Room at the Double Bamboo Temple (1073)

39 Strike your own evening drum, morning bell,
then shut the door. Lamp burning low by a solitary pillow;
gray ashes where just now you stirred the stove to red.
Lie and listen to raindrops splattering the window.

New Year's Eve: Spending the Night Outside Ch'ang-chou City (1073)

40 From the traveler, singing; from the field, weeping – both spur
     sorrow.
Fires in the distance, dipping stars move slowly toward extinction.
Am I waiting up for New Year's? Aching eyes won't close.
No one here speaks my dialect: I long for home.
A double quilt and my feet still cold – the frost must be heavy;
my head feels light – I washed it and the hair is getting thin.
I thank the flickering torch that doesn't refuse
to keep me company on a lonely boat through the night.

CROPS HAD failed, the people were starving, and Su Tung-p'o was abroad supervising
relief measures. New Year's Eve found him aboard a boat outside Ch'ang-chou, on the
Grand Canal north of Soochow.

Part Two

MIDDLE YEARS: 1074 TO 1079

Bad Wine Is Like Bad Men (1074)

DRANK with Liu Tzu-yü at Gold Mountain Temple. Got very drunk, slept on Pao-chüeh's meditation platform. Came to in the middle of the night and inscribed this on his wall.

41 Bad wine is like bad men,
    deadlier in attack than arrows or knives.
    I collapse on the platform;
    victory hopeless, truce will have to do.
    The old poet carries on bravely,
    the Zen master's words are gentle and profound.
    Too drunk to follow what they're saying,
    I'm conscious only of a red and green blur.
    I wake to find the moon sinking into the river,
    the wind rustling with a different sound.
    A lone lamp burns by the altar,
    but the two heroes – both have disappeared.

Written on Abbot Lun's Wall at Mount Chiao (1074)

42 The Master stays on Mount Chiao,
(though in fact he's never "stayed" anywhere).
No sooner had I arrived than I asked about the Way,
but the Master never said a word.
Not that he was lost for words –
he saw no reason for replying.
Then I thought, Look at your head and feet –
comfortable enough in hat and shoes, aren't they?
It's like the man with a long beard
who never worried how long it was.
But one day someone asked him,
"What do you do with it when you sleep?"
That night, pulling up the covers,
he couldn't decide if it went on top or under.
All night he tossed and turned, wondering where to put it,
till he felt like yanking it out by the roots.
These words may seem trite and shallow
but in fact they have deep meaning.
When I asked the Master what he thought,
the Master smiled his approval.

Line 2. The Master dwells in the realm of Buddhist nondualism, where relative concepts such as "staying" or "going" have no validity.

Describing Water Wheels on the Road to Wu-hsi (1074)

43 Whirling, whirling, round, round, a crow with tail in mouth;
    all lumps and bumps protruding, a snake stripped to its bones.
    Waves of emerald filling field rows, rippling like clouds;
    green needles pricking the water, rice shoots coming up.
    But in fifth month at lakeside the sands of drought fly;
    water lizards croak in their lair like the beating of yamen drums.
    Doesn't Lord Heaven see this old farmer weeping?
    Let him order A-hsiang to haul out her thunder cart!

Lines 1–2. The first line depicts the water wheel in motion, the second, the wheel at rest.

Line 6. The lizards croak in time of drought.

Line 8. According to a tale in the *Sou-shen hou-chi*, a man of Chin times was traveling along the road at nightfall when he saw a new-built grass-roofed hut by the roadside, with a woman gazing at him as he passed. He asked her for a night's lodging, which she granted. During the night he heard a young boy outside, calling and saying, "A-hsiang, the Governor says to haul out your thunder cart!" The woman excused herself and went out, and later that night there was heavy thunder and rain. Next morning when the man looked at the place where he had spent the night, he saw only a new grave.

Visiting Yung-lo Temple, I Learn that the Old Priest Wen Has Died (1074)

44 The last visit alarmed me – stork-thin, I hardly knew him;
   suddenly I learn he's gone with the clouds, no looking for him now.
   In the course of three visits, old age, sickness, death;
   in a snap of a finger, past, present, future.
   Now here, now gone – I've seen it so often I barely shed a tear,
   but my old home's hard to forget; he sticks in my thoughts.
   I must hurry to Ch'ien-t'ang, look for Yüan-tse;
   by the banks of Ko-hung River I'll wait as autumn deepens.

Lines 7–8. Reference to a tale by the Late T'ang writer Yüan Chiao that tells of two
friends, the Buddhist priest Yüan-tse and a nobleman named Li Yüan, who set off on a
trip to Mount O-mei in Szechwan. Along the way Yüan-tse suddenly announced that
the time of his death had arrived. But he said that thirteen years from then he would
meet his friend outside the T'ien-chu Temple in Hangchow (Ch'ien-t'ang) at the time
of the mid-autumn full moon. Thirteen years later Li Yüan went to the appointed
place and there on the banks of the Ko-hung River encountered a herdboy who was a
reincarnation of Yüan-tse.

Overgrown Garden Deserted in Fall (1074)

IN THE GARDEN of the Ch'en house at Hsin-ch'eng. Following the
rhymes of a poem by Ch'ao Pu-chih.

45 Overgrown garden deserted in fall,
    lonely flowers dark in the evening;
    the mountain town is far away –
    farther still, here beyond the walls.
    What did I come for?
    I stay awhile to watch cloudy peaks.
    Not finding my hardworking poet friend,
    what use is the jug of clear wine I brought?

At Twilight, Fine Rain Was Still Falling (1074)

AFTER SNOW; inscribed on North Terrace, two poems.

46 At twilight, fine rain was still falling,
the night hushed and windless, the cold getting worse.
The bedclothes felt as though they'd been drenched;
I didn't know the courtyard was piled with drifts.
Fifth watch: dawn light colors the study curtains;
under a half moon, the cold rustle of painted eaves.
I'll sweep North Terrace, have a look at Horse Ears Hill,
two peaks not yet shrouded in snow.

Ten Years – Dead and Living Dim and Draw Apart (1075)

To THE TUNE "Song of River City." The year *yi-mao*, first month, twentieth day: recording a dream I had last night.

47 Ten years – dead and living dim and draw apart.
I don't try to remember
but forgetting is hard.
Lonely grave a thousand miles off,
cold thoughts – where can I talk them out?
Even if we met you wouldn't know me,
dust on my face,
hair like frost –

In a dream last night suddenly I was home.
By the window of the little room
you were combing your hair and making up.
You turned and looked, not speaking,
only lines of tears coursing down –
year after year will it break my heart?
The moonlit grave,
its stubby pines –

WRITTEN at Mi-chou in 1075. The dream was of the poet's first wife, Wang Fu, whom he married in 1054, when she was fifteen. She died in 1065, and the following year, when the poet's father died, he carried her remains back to his old home in Szechwan and buried them in the family plot, planting a number of little pine trees around the grave mound.

Children (1075)

48 Children don't know what worry means!
Stand up to go and they hang on my clothes.
I'm about to scold them
but my wife eggs them on in their silliness:
"The children are silly but you're much worse!
What good does all this worrying do?"
Stung by her words, I go back to my seat.
She rinses a wine cup to put before me.
How much better than Liu Ling's wife,
grumbling at the cost of her husband's drinking!

Line 9. "Liu Ling's wife." Liu Ling was a poet of the Chin Dynasty and one of the Seven Sages of the Bamboo Grove who flourished in the middle of the third century A.D. According to a version of the story, his wife begged him to give up drinking for the sake of his health. He protested that he was too weak-willed to give it up alone, and could do so only if she would prepare offerings of wine and meat so that he might take a temperance vow before the gods. When she had done this, he delivered this prayer:

> Heaven gave birth to Liu Ling,
>   gave him the name of Wine.
> One gallon at a gulp,
>   five quarts for a hangover.
> The words of a woman –
>   take care not to heed them!

He then helped himself to the offerings and was soon as drunk as ever.

Bright Moon, When Did You Appear? (1076)

To THE TUNE of "Prelude to Water Music." On mid-autumn night of the year *ping-ch'en* (1076) I drank merrily until dawn, got very drunk and wrote this poem, all the while thinking longingly of Tzu-yu.

49   Bright moon, when did you appear?
Lifting my wine, I question the blue sky.
Tonight in the palaces and halls of heaven
what year is it, I wonder?
I would like to ride the wind, make my home there,
only I fear in porphyry towers, under jade eaves,
in those high places the cold wind would be more than I could bear.
So I rise and dance and play in your pure beams,
though this human world – how can it vie with yours?

Circling red chambers,
low in the curtained door,
you light our sleeplessness.
Surely you bear us no ill will –
why then must you be so round at times when we humans are parted!
People have their griefs and joys, their togetherness and separation,
the moon its dark and clear times, its roundings and wanings.
I only hope we two may have long long lives,
may share the moon's beauty, though a thousand miles apart.

Pear Blossoms by the Eastern Palisade
(1077)

50 Pear blossoms pale white, willows deep green —
when willow fluff scatters, falling blossoms will fill the town.
Snowy boughs by the eastern palisade set me pondering —
in a lifetime how many springs do we see?

The New Year's Eve Blizzard Kept Me from Leaving (1077)

I WAS DETAINED by a heavy snow at Wei-chou on New Year's Eve, but on the morning of the first day it cleared and I resumed my journey. Along the way, it started to snow again.

51   The New Year's Eve blizzard kept me from leaving;
on the first, clear skies see me off.
The east wind blows away last night's drunk;
on a lean horse, I nod in the remains of a dream.
Dim and hazy, the dawn light breaks through;
fluttering and turning, the last flakes fall.
I dismount and pour myself a drink in the field —
delicious — but who to share it with?
All at once evening clouds close down,
tumbling flurries that show no break.
Flakes big as goose feathers hang from the horse's mane
till I think I'm riding a great white bird.
Three years' drought plagues the east;
roofs sag on house rows, their owners fled.
The old farmer lays aside his plow and sighs,
gulps tears that burn his starving guts.
Spring snow falls late this year
but spring wheat can still be planted.
Do I grumble at the trials of official travel?
To help you I'll sing a song of good harvest.

Reading the Poetry of Meng Chiao: Two Poems (1078)

52 Night: reading Meng Chiao's poems,
    characters fine as cow's hair.
    By the cold lamp, my eyes blur and swim.
    Good passages I rarely find –
    lone flowers poking up from the mud –
    but more hard words than the *Odes* or *Li sao* –
    jumbled rocks clogging the clear stream,
    making rapids too swift for poling.
    My first impression is of eating little fishes –
    what you get's not worth the trouble;
    or of boiling tiny mud crabs
    and ending up with some empty claws.
    For refinement he might compete with monks
    but he'll never match his master Han Yü.
    Man's life is like morning dew,
    a flame eating up the oil night by night.
    Why should I strain my ears
    listening to the squeaks of this autumn insect?
    Better lay aside the book
    and drink my cup of jade-white wine.

MENG CHIAO (751-814), a well known T'ang poet, was a disciple of the even better known poet and statesman, Han Yü (768-824). Su was probably reading a printed edition of the so-called small character variety.

Along the Road to Stone Lake (1078)

To THE TUNE of "Wash Stream Sands." Five poems written along the road to Stone Lake at Hsü-chou, where I went to give thanks for rain. The lake is twenty li east of the city. Though separated from the Ssu River, its water level is always the same as that of the river and its water of the same degree of clearness or muddiness.

53   Throw on rouge and powder, watch the governor pass!
In threes and fives by thorn hedge gates,
they push and trample each other's red silk skirts.

Lead the old, bring the children! Like a harvest festival,
crows and hawks wheeling above the village shrine –
at dusk I met an old man lying drunk beside the road.

54   Layer on layer of hemp leaves, jute leaves shining;
some family is boiling cocoons – the whole village smells good.
Beyond the hedge, "spinning girls" call invitingly.

White-haired, with goosefoot staff, he raises drunken eyes –
pick greens, grind parched grain, ease an empty belly!
Tell me, when will bean leaves turn yellow here?

55   Flutter, flutter, on clothes and cap, jujube flowers fall;
village south, village north echo to spinning reels.
Half leaning on the old willow, they peddle yellow melons.

Wine-drowsy, a long road, I'm getting sleepier;
sun high, throat parched, thinking only of tea–
I'll knock on a gate and see what the villagers'll give me.

56 Soft grasses, a plain of sedge fresh with passing rain;
horses race the light sand road but raise no dust.
When can I quit and take up plowing and planting?

Sun warm on mulberry and hemp glints like water;
wind over mugwort and moxa comes perfumed.
Your governor, long ago, lived in a place like this.

THERE WAS a drought this year and the poet, in his capacity of governor, had gone to
Stone Lake, said by local lore to be the home of a rain-making dragon, to pray for rain.
When rain fell, he made a second trip to give thanks.

Mid-Autumn Moon (1078)

57 Six years the moon shone at mid-autumn;
   five years it saw us parted.
   I sing your farewell song;
   sobs from those who sit with me.
   The southern capital must be busy,
   but you won't let the occasion pass:
   Hundred-league lake of melted silver,
   thousand-foot towers in the pendant mirror –
   at third watch, when songs and flutes are stilled
   and figures blur in the clear shade of trees,
   you return to your north hall rooms,
   cold light glinting on the dew of leaves;
   calling for wine, you drink with your wife
   and tell the children stories, thinking of me.
   You have no way of knowing I've been sick,
   that I face the pears and chestnuts, cup empty,
   and stare east of the old riverbed
   where buckwheat blossoms spread their snow.
   I wanted to write a verse to your last year's song
   but I was afraid my heart would break.

Line 8. "Pendant mirror." Poetic term for the moon. The poem is addressed to Su's brother, Tzu-yu.

Climbing Cloud Dragon Mountain (1078)

58 Drunk, I race up Yellow Grass Hill,
   slope strewn with boulders like flocks of sheep,
   at the top collapse on a bed of stone,
   staring at white clouds in a bottomless sky.
   My song sinks to the valley on long autumn winds.
   Passers-by look up, gaze southeast,
   clap their hands and laugh: "The governor's gone mad!"

Hundred Pace Rapids (1078)

WHEN Wang Ting-kuo was visiting me at P'eng-ch'eng [Hsü-chou], he went one day in a small boat, accompanied by Yen Ch'ang-tao and three singing girls, P'an, Ying, and Ch'ing, for an outing on the Ssu River. To the north they climbed Holy Woman Hill, southward they poled down the Hundred Pace Rapids, playing flutes, drinking wine, and returning home by moonlight. I had business to attend to and could not go with them, but when evening came and I had changed into informal Taoist robes, I stood at the top of the Yellow Tower and gazed in the direction they had gone, laughing and thinking to myself that not since the poet Li Po died some three hundred years ago had there been such a merry expedition. Wang Ting-kuo went away, and the following month Master Ts'an-liao and I poled down those same rapids, thinking of that earlier outing, which now seemed like an event of the distant past. Sighing to myself, I made these two poems. One I gave to Ts'an-liao, and the other I sent to Wang Ting-kuo, and I have shown them to Yen Ch'ang-tao and Shu Yao-wen and urged them to write on the same theme.

59   Long rapids drop steeply, waves leap up;
the light boat shoots south like a plunging shuttle.
Water birds fly up at the boatman's cry;
the thread of water pushes through tangled rocks.
We're like a rabbit darting from preying hawks,
a fine horse racing down a thousand-foot slope,
a string snapping from a lute, an arrow from a bow,
lightning glimpsed through a crack, a raindrop rolling off a lotus leaf.
The four hills swirl around me, wind stops my ears;
I see only the current boiling in a thousand whirlpools.
Enjoying an hour of delight among these cliffs,
I'm like the river god boasting of autumn floods.
I give in to the change that advances day and night;
sit, and in a moment of thought fly beyond Silla.

Men in drunken dreams wrangle and steal,
never believing that thorns will bury the bronze camels.
In this reverie I lose a thousand kalpas;
I stare at the water: it moves with unspeakable slowness.
See there, on the face of the green rock bank –
holes like hornets' nests where ancient boatmen braced their poles!
Only make sure the mind never clings!
The Creator may hurry us, but what can we do?
Turn the boat around, mount horse, and go home.
Master Ts'an-liao complains I talk too much!

Line 12. "Autumn floods." A reference to *Chuang Tzu*, Sec. 17, *Ch'iu-shui* chapter, the story of how the god of the Yellow River, intoxicated by the might of the river when it was swollen by autumn rains, boasted of his power, until he came face to face with the sea and realized his relative insignificance.

Line 16. "Bronze camels." Camels, cast in the Han dynasty, that stood by the palace gate at Loyang. A scholar of the Chin, So Ching (239-303), was famous for having pointed at the camels and predicted that they would one day be buried in a tangle of thorns.

On a Boat, Awake at Night (1079)

60 Faint wind rustles reeds and cattails;
    I open the hatch, expecting rain – moon floods the lake.
    Boatmen and water birds dream the same dream;
    a big fish splashes off like a frightened fox.
    It's late – men and creatures forget each other
    while my shadow and I amuse ourselves alone.
    Dark tides creep over the flats – I pity the cold mud-worms;
    the setting moon, caught in a willow, lights a dangling spider.
    Life passes swiftly, hedged by sorrow;
    how long before you've lost it – a scene like this?
    Cocks crow, bells ring, a hundred birds scatter;
    drums pound from the bow, shout answers shout.

Line 12. "Drums." Drums were sounded in the bow when the boat was under way.

Held Up Two Days at Gold Mountain (1079)

61 The bell on the pagoda top talks to itself:
high winds tomorrow – no river-crossing!
Morning, and white waves pound the green bank,
dashing showers of spray up to our window.
Hundred-weight ships don't dare put out
but a fishing boat – one leaf – bounces along.
Come to think of it, why rush to town?
I laugh at rain dragons – who are they angry at?
The servants may wonder why I stay so long
but my family will forgive me with wind like this!
The monk of Ch'ien-shan – what's he doing?
Past midnight, up alone, listening for gruel call –

Line 12. "Gruel call." A wooden sounding board called the monks to their breakfast of gruel. Su's friend Ts'an-liao ("the monk of Ch'ien-shan") was probably spending the night in meditation.

Lotus Viewing (1079)

WITH THE Wang brothers and my son Mai, went around the city looking at lotus flowers. We climbed to the pavilion on Mount Hsien, and in the evening went to the Temple of Flying Petals. We assigned rhymes for poems; I was given *yüeh, ming, hsing,* and *hsi,* and wrote four poems.

62   The clear wind – what is it?
     Something to be loved, not to be named,
     moving like a prince wherever it goes;
     the grass and trees whisper its praise.
     This outing of ours never had a purpose;
     let the lone boat swing about as it will.
     In the middle of the current, lying face up,
     I greet the breeze that happens along
     and lift a cup to offer to the vastness:
     how pleasant – that we have no thought for each other!
     Coming back through two river valleys,
     clouds and water shine in the night.

63   Clerks and townsmen pity my laziness;
     day by day I have fewer disputes to settle.
     So I can go drinking and wandering around,
     even spending a whole night out.
     We come looking for the Temple of Flying Petals,
     making the most of the light that's left.
     A bell ringing; the sound of gathering feet:
     monks tumble out in mountain robes.
     I may be dropping by at odd hours –
     with foot and cane I'll open the door myself.
     Don't treat me like a high official!
     Outside I look like one, but inside I'm not.

Under the Heaven of Our Holy Ruler (1079)

BECAUSE OF what has happened, I have been confined to the imperial censorate prison. The prison officials treat me with increasing harshness, and I doubt that I can stand it much longer. If I die in prison, I will have no chance to say goodby to Tzu-yu, and therefore I wrote these two poems and gave them to the warden, Liang Hsü, to deliver to him.

64 Under the heaven of our holy ruler, all things turn to spring,
    but I in dark ignorance have destroyed myself.
    Before my hundred years are past, I'm called to settle up;
    my leaderless family, ten mouths, must be your worry now.
    Bury me anywhere on the green hills
    and another year in night rain grieve for me alone.
    Let us be brothers in lives and lives to come,
    mending then the bonds that this world breaks.

IN 1079, five months after he had assumed his duties as governor of Hu-chou, the poet was arrested and taken to the capital on charges of "slandering the emperor," i.e., criticizing the measures adopted by Wang An-shih and his successors in the New Laws party. There Su was subjected to severe examination in order to determine what degree of covert satire was intended in his poems. This, the first of the two poems of farewell to Tzu-yu, was written late in the year, during his imprisonment.

A Hundred Days, Free to Go (1080)

TWELFTH MONTH, twenty-eighth day. I receive the favor of being appointed special supernumerary of the Water Bureau and second officer in the home guard at Huang-chou: two poems.

65   A hundred days, free to go, and it's almost spring;
for the years left, pleasure will be my chief concern.
Out the gate, I do a dance, wind blows my face;
our galloping horses race along as magpies cheer.
I face the wine cup and it's all a dream,
pick up a poem brush, already inspired.
Why try to fix the blame for trouble past?
Years now I've stolen posts I never should have had.

WRITTEN on his release from prison on the last day of the year (early 1080), after a confinement of 130 days. The posts to which he was appointed were minor and nominal; in fact he was being banished to the region of Huang-chou in Hupeh, on the north bank of the Yangtze.

Line 3. "I do a dance." According to another interpretation of these two words, "I stop to piss."

Part Three

On First Arriving at Huang-chou (1080)

66 Funny – I never could keep my mouth shut;
   it gets worse the older I grow.
   The long river loops the town – fish must be tasty;
   good bamboo lines the hills – smell the fragrant shoots!
   An exile, why mind being a supernumerary?
   Other poets have worked for the Water Bureau.
   Too bad I was no help to the government
   but still they pay me in old wine sacks.

Line 8. "Wine sacks." Wine was a government monopoly under the Sung, and lesser officials were sometimes paid off in old sacks that had been used for squeezing wine, which could be sold or bartered.

A Letter From Huang-chou (1080?)

67 When I first arrived in Huang-chou, I was very much worried about
how I would get along, since my salary had been cut off and my house-
hold is a fairly large one. However, by practicing the strictest economy,
we manage to spend no more than 150 cash a day. On the first of each
month, I get out 4,500 cash and divide it up into 30 bundles, which I
then hang from the rafters of the ceiling. Every morning I take the pic-
ture-hanging rod and fish down one bundle, and then I put the rod
away. I also keep a large section of bamboo in which I put anything left
over at the end of the day so I will have something to entertain visitors
with. This is a method my friend Chia Yün-lao taught me. I figure I
still have enough money left to last us a year or more, and after that
we'll think of something else. Running water digs a ditch – there's no
need to worry about things ahead of time. So you see I don't really
have a single care on my mind.

On the opposite bank of the river from where I am is the wonderful
scenery of Wu-ch'ang. There is a man from Shu named Wang who
lives in the town there, and very often when I am over visiting him the
wind comes up and the waves make it impossible for me to get back
home. Mr. Wang kills a chicken, cooks some millet for me, and doesn't
get annoyed even if I stay three or four days. Also there is Mr. P'an who
runs a wine store at the landing at Fan-k'ou. I can climb into a little
boat and row right across the river to the foot of his store. It's local
wine made in the village, of course, but very good. There are enor-
mous quantities of tangerines and small persimmons, and huge taros
that grow over a foot long, fully as large as those we had in Shu. Rice
comes from other districts but costs only 20 cash a measure because it
can be brought in by water. Lamb is as good as that up north, and pork,
beef, and venison are dirt cheap. Fish and crabs too cost next to noth-
ing. Hu Ting-chih, who is supervisor of the wine bureau over at Ch'i-
ting, has brought a great many books with him and is delighted to lend
them to people. There are several officials in Huang-chou, all of whom
have excellent kitchens and enjoy giving parties.

From all this you can see that I'm really very well taken care of, don't you think? There are any number of things I'd like to say to you, but I'm coming to the end of the paper. I can imagine you reading this far and now pulling back your whiskers and chuckling.

EXCERPT from a letter written probably around the eleventh month of 1080 and addressed to the poet's friend and disciple, Ch'in Kuan (1049-1101). Some eight hundred of Su's letters survive.

Ten Days of Spring Cold Kept Me Indoors (1081)

ON THE TWENTIETH DAY of the first month I set off for Ch'i-ting. Three friends from the district, P'an, Ku, and Kuo, saw me off at the Ch'an-chuang Monastery east of Nü-wang-ch'eng.

68   Ten days of spring cold kept me indoors;
I didn't know willows were budding in the village.
In the frozen valley, a stream gurgles faintly;
sheets of green hide burnt stubble in the fields.
A few acres of poor land hold me here;
warming half a jug of cloudy wine, I wait for you.
A year ago today I crossed the mountain pass —
fine rain on plum flowers nearly broke my spirit.

Eastern Slope (1081)

EASTERN SLOPE: eight poems with introduction. For two years after coming to Huang-chou, my hardship and poverty increased day by day until a friend, Ma Cheng-ch'ing, distressed by the fact that I wasn't getting enough to eat, asked the district administration to give me the use of several tens of *mou* of land which had formerly been an army camp, so that I could cultivate it for myself. The land had been left untouched for a long time, and was no more than a waste of brambles, stones, and broken tiles. In addition it was a year of severe drought. I came near to exhausting every ounce of muscle and energy I had opening it up for cultivation, and letting go the plow with a sigh, I wrote these poems to console myself in my labors. Perhaps in years to come the harvest will be such that I will forget the hard work I put into it.

69 Abandoned earthworks nobody tends,
collapsed wall tangled in vines –
who'd waste strength on land like this?
Work all year for no return.
But here's a stranger, alone,
heaven against him, nowhere to go,
pitching in to clear the rubble and wrack.
Weather too dry, soil lean:
pushing through brambles and weeds,
wondering can I scrape out a handful of produce,
I sigh and let go the plow –
my barn – when will I fill it up?

70 Waste fields buried in bush,
but high and low will have a use.
Damp lowland – plant rice there;
jujubes and chestnuts on the eastern rise.
My Shu friend south of the river

has already promised mulberry seeds;
good bamboo's not hard to grow
(only watch it doesn't spread out of hand).
Now to choose the best site,
the safest place to build my house.
The boy burning off old dead grass
races to tell me he's found a well.
It's too soon to promise a hearty meal,
but we know where to fill our drinking gourds!

71   A little stream used to cross my land,
came from the mountain pass back there,
under city walls, through villages —
the current sluggish and choked with grass —
feeding finally into K'o Clan Pond,
ten *mou* stocked with fish and shrimp.
Drought this year dried it up,
its cracked bed plastered with brown duckweed.
Last night clouds came from hills to the south;
rain soaked the ground a plowshare deep.
Rivulets found the channel again,
knowing I'd chopped back the weeds.
In the mud a few old roots of cress
still alive from a year ago.
If white buds will open again,
when spring doves come I'll make a stew!

72   I planted rice before Spring Festival
and already I'm counting joys!
Rainy skies darken the spring pond;
by green-bladed paddies I chat with friends.
Transplanting takes till the first of summer,
delight growing with wind-blown stalks.
The moon looks down on dew-wet leaves
strung one by one with hanging pearls.
Fall comes and frosty ears grow heavy,

topple, and lean propped on each other.
From banks and dikes I hear only
a sound of locusts like wind and rain.
Rice, newly hulled, goes to the steamer,
grains of jade that light up the basket.
A long time I've eaten only government fare,
old rusty rice no better than mud.
Now to taste something new –
I've already promised my mouth and belly.

73   A good farmer hates to wear out the land;
I'm lucky this plot was ten years fallow.
It's too soon to count on mulberries;
my best bet is a crop of wheat.
I planted seed and within the month
dirt on the rows was showing green.
An old farmer warned me,
don't let the seedlings shoot up too fast!
If you want plenty of dumpling flour
turn a cow or sheep in here to graze.
Good advice – I bowed my thanks;
I won't forget you when my belly's full.

74   Plant jujubes and in time I can pick them;
plant pine and in time it can be cut.
I'll have to wait ten years or more,
but I did right to put them in.
After all, what's ten years
when a thousand pass like hail on the wind?
I've heard of Li Heng's "slaves";
his is the best plan to follow.
A friend who was an official with me,
now at a post in Ch'ien-yüeh,
sent me oranges three inches across –
they lit up the whole room with their shining.
If he'd get me a hundred seedlings,

I'd plant them in spring when ice is thick.
I see it now — beyond the bamboo hedge,
green and yellow dangling by the roof tips.

THE FIRST SIX POEMS in the series of eight. The poet gave the name "Tung-p'o" or "Eastern Slope" to his plot of ground, and later used it as his *hao* or literary name; hence he is commonly referred to as Su Tung-p'o. Since one *mou* was equal to one sixth of an acre, Su's plot probably measured about five acres. It seems to have been some distance from the house where he was staying, which was at a place called Lin-kao, overlooking the Yangtze.

71, line 16. "Spring doves." A note by the poet explains that stew made of dove meat and cress buds is a favorite dish in his native region of Szechwan.

72, line 1. "Spring Festival." Ch'ing-ming, the festival held on the 106th day after the winter solstice.

74, line 7. "Li Heng's slaves." Li Heng of the kingdom of Wu (early third century A.D.) left his heirs an orchard of a thousand orange trees, explaining in his will that they were "a thousand wooden slaves" that would earn for his descendants a comfortable living.

Drank Tonight at Eastern Slope (1082)

To THE TUNE of "The Immortal by the River." Coming home at night to Lin-kao.

75 Drank tonight at Eastern Slope, sobered up, drank again;
got home somewhere around third watch.
The houseboy snores like thunder;
I bang the gate but nobody answers.
Leaning on my stick, I listen to river sounds.

Always it irks me – this body not my own.
When can I forget the world's business?
Night far gone, wind still, river creped in ripples:
I'll leave here in a little boat,
on far waters spend the years remaining.

Lines 9-10. Because of these last two lines, it is said, a rumor spread around that the poet had actually gotten into a boat in the night and disappeared. The governor of Huang-chou, who was responsible for seeing that Su did not leave the district, rushed in alarm to the poet's house, to find him in bed snoring. Word of his supposed escape even reached Emperor Shen-tsung in the capital.

Two Prose Poems on the Red Cliff (1082)
First Prose Poem

76 In the autumn of the year *jen-hsü*, the seventh month, when the moon had just passed its prime, some friends and I went out in a small boat to amuse ourselves at the foot of the Red Cliff.[1] A fresh breeze blew softly across the water, leaving the waves unruffled. As I picked up the wine jar and poured a drink for my friends, I hummed a poem to the moon and sang a phrase on its strange beauty.

In a little while, the moon rose from the eastern hills and wandered across the sky between the Archer and the Goat. White dew settled over the river, and its shining surface reached to the sky. Letting the boat go where it pleased, we drifted over the immeasurable fields of water. I felt a boundless exhilaration, as though I were sailing on the void or riding the wind and didn't know where to stop. I was filled with a lightness, as though I had left the world and were standing alone, or had sprouted wings and were flying up to join the immortals. As I drank the wine, my delight increased and, thumping the edge of the boat, I composed a song that went:

> With cassia sweep and
> Oars of orchid wood,
> Strike the empty moon,
> Row through its drifting light.
> Thoughts fly far away –
> I long for my loved one
> In a corner of the sky.

One friend began to play on an open flute, following my song and harmonizing with it. The flute made a wailing sound, as though the player were filled with resentment or longing, or were lamenting or protesting. Long notes trailed through the night like endless threads

---

1. A steep escarpment overlooking the Yangtze near Huang-chou.

of silk, a sound to make dragons dance in hidden caves, or to set the widow weeping in her lonely boat.

Saddened by his playing, I straightened my robe, bowed and asked, "What makes you play this way?"

He replied,

> "'The moon is bright, stars grow few,
> Crows and magpies fly to the south.'

That's how Ts'ao Ts'ao's poem goes, doesn't it?[2] There you can see Hsia-k'ou to the west, Wu-ch'ang to the east. A dense tangle of dark green, bounded by mountains and river – this is the very spot where the young Chou Yü swooped down on Ts'ao Ts'ao, isn't it? After Ts'ao Ts'ao had conquered Ching and taken Chiang-ling, he sailed down the Yangtze to the east. The stems and sterns of his ships touched for a thousand miles, and his flags and pennants blocked out the sky. He drank wine overlooking the river, laid his lance across the saddle, and wrote his poems. Surely he was the greatest hero of his time – yet where is he now?

"What then of you and me? Fishermen and wood gatherers by the banks of streams, companions to fish and crayfish, friends of deer and elk, riding this leaf of a boat, dipping gourds into the wine jar and pouring for each other – we are no more than summer flies between heaven and earth, a grain of millet on the waste of the sea! It grieves me that life is so short, and I envy the long river that never stops. If we could only link arms with the flying immortals and wander where we please, embrace the moon and grow old with it.... But I know that such hopes cannot quickly be fulfilled, and so I confide these lingering notes to the sad air."

---

2. The lines are quoted from a poem written by Ts'ao Ts'ao (155–220), military dictator of the region of Wei. Su's friend then goes on to recall Ts'ao Ts'ao's famous battle with his rivals, Liu Pei, Sun Chüan, Chou Yü, and others. The battle took place in A.D. 208, at a spot on the Yangtze called Red Cliff, and resulted in a disastrous defeat for Ts'ao Ts'ao. Because of its fame, many other spots on the Yangtze came to be called Red Cliff; the one where the poet and his friends are spending the evening is not the actual site of the battle but is considerably farther down the river.

I asked, "Do you know how it is with the water and the moon? 'The water flows on and on like this,'[3] but somehow it never flows away. The moon waxes and wanes, and yet in the end it's the same moon. If we look at things through the eyes of change, then there's not an instant of stillness in all creation. But if we observe the changelessness of things, then we and all beings alike have no end. What is there to be envious about?

"Moreover, everything in the world has its owner, and if a thing doesn't belong to us, we don't dare take a hair of it. Only the clear breeze over the river, or the bright moon between the hills, which our ears hear as music, our eyes see beauty in – these we may take without prohibition, these we may make free with and they will never be used up. These are the endless treasures of the Creator, here for you and me to enjoy together!"

My friend was pleased and, laughing, washed the wine cups and filled them up again. But the fruit and other things we had brought to eat were all gone and so, among the litter of cups and bowls, we lay down in a heap in the bottom of the boat, unaware that the east was already growing light.

---

3. A quotation from *Analects* IX, 16: "The Master was standing by a river and said, 'The water flows on and on like this, never stopping day or night.'"

Second Prose Poem

77 This same year, on the fifteenth day of the tenth month, I was walking back from Snow Hall to my home at Lin-kao.[1] Two friends were with me, and we went by way of Yellow Mud Slope. Frost had already fallen and the trees were bare of leaves. Our shadows appeared on the ground, and looking up, we saw that the moon had risen. Glancing around to enjoy the sight, we walked along singing songs back and forth.

After a while, I sighed and said, "Here I have guests and there's no wine! And even if I had some wine, there's nothing to eat with it. A clear moon, a fresh breeze – what will we do with such a fine night?"

"Today at sundown," said one of my friends, "I put out a net and caught some fish with big mouths and delicate scales, like the perch of Pine River. And there must be somewhere we can get some wine...."

As soon as I got home, I consulted my wife. "I have a gallon of wine that's been put away for a long time," she said. "I was saving it for some occasion when you might suddenly need it."

So we took the wine and fish and went for another trip to the foot of the Red Cliff. The river raced along noisily, its sheer banks rising a thousand feet. The mountains were very high, the moon small. The level of the water had fallen, leaving boulders sticking out. How much time had passed since my last visit? I couldn't recognize them as the same river and hills!

Tucking up my robe, I began to climb, picking my way along the steep embankment, pushing through tangled grass, straddling rocks the shape of tigers, clambering over roots twisted like dragons. I pulled my way up to the eagle's precarious nest, and looked down into the hidden halls of the river god. My two friends couldn't keep up.

I gave a long, shrill whoop. Trees and grass shook and swayed, the

---

1. Snow Hall was a small house on Eastern Slope which the poet built early in 1082 and where he sometimes stayed, though his wife and family continued to live in the house at Lin-kao. He completed it just at the time of a heavy snow, hence the name.

mountains rang, the valley echoed. A wind came up, roiling the water, and I felt a chill of sadness, a shrinking fear. I knew with a shudder that I couldn't stay there any longer.

I went back to my friends and got into the boat, and we turned it loose to drift with the current, content to let it stop wherever it chose. The night was half over and all around was deserted and still, when a lone crane appeared, cutting across the river from the east. Its wings looked like cart wheels, and it wore a black robe and a coat of white silk. With a long, grating cry, it swooped over our boat and went off to the west.

Soon afterwards, I left my friends and went to bed. I dreamed I saw a Taoist immortal in a feather robe come bouncing down the road past the foot of Lin-kao. He bowed to me and said, "Did you enjoy your outing to the Red Cliff?" I asked him his name, but he looked down and didn't answer.

"Ah, wait – of course – now I know! Last evening, flying over our boat and crying – that was you, wasn't it?"

He turned his head and laughed, and I woke up with a start. I opened the door and peered out, but I could see no sign of him.

Rain at the Time of Cold Food (1082)

78 Since coming to Huang-chou,
    this is my third Cold Food festival.
    Each year I hate to see spring go,
    but it goes anyway, heeding no regrets.
    On top of that, this year we're pestered with rain;
    two months now it's been bleak as fall.
    I lie and listen to cherry apple blossoms,
    pale pink snow getting dirty in the mud.
    Of forces that steal things away in the dark,
    the most powerful comes in the middle of the night,
    as though a young man were to take to bed sick,
    then rise from his sickbed to find his hair gone gray.

COLD FOOD, which comes 105 days after the winter solstice, is a spring festival celebrated by a meal of various foods eaten cold.

Lines 7-12. The lines in which the rain carrying off the cherry apple blossoms is likened to a thief in the night allude to the passage in *Chuang Tzu* Sec. 6: "You hide your boat in the ravine and your fish net in the swamp and tell yourself they will be safe. But in the middle of the night a strong man shoulders them and carries them off, and in your stupidity you don't know why it happened."

South Hall (1083)

79 Sweep the floor, burn incense, close the door to sleep;
a mat marked like water, curtains like mist.
I dream a guest comes, wake wondering where I am,
prop open the west window on waves that meet the sky.

THE FIFTH of five poems with this title written in the summer of 1083. The previous year, a friend, Ts'ai Ch'eng-hsi, traveling through Huang-chou on official business, had had a little three-room addition built onto the poet's house at Lin-kao, which overlooked the Yangtze, in order to make him more comfortable. It was called South Hall.

Line 2. Mats of woven bamboo or rush were spread on the beds in summer for cooler sleeping.

To the Tune of "Partridge Sky" (1083?)

80 Mountains shine through forest breaks, bamboo hides the wall;
    withered grass by small ponds, jumbled cicada cries.
    White birds again and again cut across the sky;
    faint scent of lotus shining pink on the water.

    Beyond the village,
    by old town walls,
    with goosefoot cane I stroll where late sunlight turns.
    Thanks to rain that fell at the third watch last night
    I get another cool day in this floating life.

Beginning of Autumn: A Poem to Send to Tzu-yu (1083)

81 The hundred rivers day and night flow on,
    we and all things following;
    only the heart remains unmoved,
    clutching the past.
    I recall when we stayed at Huai-yüan Stop,
    door shut against fall heat,
    eating boiled greens, studying,
    wiping away the sweat, you and I.
    The west wind suddenly turned cold;
    dried leaves blew in the window.
    You got up for a heavier coat
    and took hold of my hand:
    We won't be young for long –
    I needn't tell you.
    Probably we'll have to part,
    hard to tell when success may come –
    even then I felt a chill of sorrow,
    and now when both of us are old –
    too late to look for a lost road,
    too late, I'm afraid, to study the Way.
    This fall I began talks to buy some land;
    if I build a house, it should be done by spring.
    Nights at Snow Hall, in wind and rain,
    already I hear you talking to me.

THE POET had abandoned all hope of resuming his official career, and in the previous year had begun to look around for a place to buy land and retire for the rest of his life. His brother Tzu-yu, implicated in the slander charges brought against Su, had been exiled in 1081 to Yün-chou in Kiangsu, where he held a minor post as supervisor of the government salt and wine bureau.

Line 5. "Huai-yüan Stop." An inn at the post station outside the south gate of K'ai-feng. The time was 1060, and Su Tung-p'o and his brother were preparing for the special examination which, successfully passed the following year, launched them on their careers as government officials and brought about their long separation.

Eastern Slope (1083)

82 Rain has washed Eastern Slope, the moon shines clear;
where townsmen walked earlier, farmers pass.
Why mind jagged stones on the hillside path?
I like the ringing sound my stick makes when it strikes.

Part Four

RETURN: 1084 TO 1093

Presented to Abbot Ch'ang-tsung of the East Forest Temple (1084)

83   Voice of the valley stream – this is his long broad tongue;
the color of the hills – is it not his clean pure body?
Last night you mastered eighty-four thousand verses;
another day how will you explain them to others?

WRITTEN on a visit to the Tung-lin-ssu or East Forest Temple of Mount Lu. The poem is preserved in the *Leng-chai yeh-hua* or *Evening Discourses from a Cold Studio* by the Ch'an monk Hui-hung (1071-1128) and is said to be Su's "enlightenment verse," the expression of his understanding of the ultimate truth of Buddhism. It has had an enormous influence on later Chinese and Japanese Ch'an or Zen literature.

Line 1–2. The sutras often speak of the Buddha's "long broad tongue," which is symbolic of his eloquence and the truth of the words he speaks. They likewise refer often to his "clean pure body."

Written on the Wall at West Forest Temple (1084)

84 From the side, a whole range; from the end, a single peak;
far, near, high, low, no two parts alike.
Why can't I tell the true shape of Lu-shan?
Because I myself am in the mountain.

IN THE THIRD MONTH of this year, the poet was ordered to move to Ju-chou in Honan, an indication that his sentence had been lightened and he was free to move beyond the confines of Huang-chou. Before proceeding to Ju-chou, he crossed the Yangtze and traveled south to visit his brother in Yün-chou. West Forest Temple was in Kiangsi at Lu-shan or Mount Lu, famous for its scenery and as a center of Buddhist activity from early times. The poet stayed at the mountain for a few days on his way to Yün-chou.

Three Hundred Tiers of Green Hills (1084)

ON THE WAY from Hsing-kuo to Yün-chou. Spent the night at a
farm house twenty-five li south of Stone Field Station.

85   Three hundred tiers of green hills above the valley;
man on a fast horse, thin robe flying, sketched in one stroke.
Houses there where tall bamboo banks the hill;
a clear stream cuts the road — it knew I was thirsty.
Straw sandals hang loose, bamboo staff is light;
rush mat feels cool, bed smells of pine.
In the early hours, wind and dew fill the courtyard
where a lone firefly flashes on and off.

Painting of a Wild Goose by the Scholar in Retirement Ch'en Chih-kung of Kao-yu (1084)

86   When a wild goose spies a human being,
      its whole bearing changes even before it flies off.
      What spot did you observe it from
      to capture this air of unconcern,
      the form like a stick of dried wood,
      both painter and bird utterly at ease!
      North wind shakes the dry reeds,
      light snow falls in glimmering flakes.
      Clouds and water grow dark and sullen,
      chips of rock and sand gleam faintly.
      Crestfallen, the hunter with his stringed arrows gives up,
      as the bird wings away to far off rivers and seas.

New Year's Eve (1084)

NEW YEAR'S EVE at Ssu-chou; snow. Huang Shih-shih sent us a present of cream and wine.

87 Twilight snow whirls down handfuls of powdered rice;
spring river whispers over yellow sand.
Past visits – dreams to be recounted only.
An exile is like a monk: where is home?
Before I can write, ink on the cold slab freezes;
lone lamp – I wonder why? – forms a flower.
In the middle of the night you send us cream and wine.
I jump up in surprise, my wife and children laugh and shout.

Line 6. "Flower." The formation of a so-called snuff flower – a peculiar twisting of the wick – was believed to be a lucky omen.

Mirage at Sea (1085)

FOR A LONG TIME I have heard of the mirage to be seen off the coast of Teng-chou. The elders of the place told me that it usually appeared in spring or summer, and since I arrived so late in the year, there was little hope I could see it now. Five days after I reached my new post, I was ordered to leave, and I was very annoyed at having had no chance to see the mirage, so I went to pray at the shrine of the Sea God, the King of Broad Virtue. The next day I saw the mirage and wrote this poem.

88 To the east, clouds and sea: emptiness on emptiness;
and do immortals come and go in that bright void?
From undulations of the floating world all forms are born,
but no gates of cowrie locked on palaces of pearl –
it is all illusion! My mind knows,
but my eyes dare plead to see the god's invention:
cold days, icy sea – though heaven and earth are sealed,
consent for my sake to rouse your sleeping dragons!
Banked towers, blue-green hills rise in the frosty dawn—
the mirage! a wonder to astound the elders.
In this world, all is won by human strength alone;
beyond the world is nothing. Who works these wonders?
I blurted out a plea and it was not denied;
troubles too must be man-made and not a blight from Heaven.
When the governor of Ch'ao-yang turned north from exile
he rejoiced to see the piled-up crests of Mount Heng,
claiming his honest heart had moved mountain spirits
(unaware the Creator merely pitied his old age).
He had his delight – not easy to come by;
the gods rewarded him richly too.
Late sun, a lone bird lost in boundless distance:
I see only green sea – a buffed bronze mirror.

This new poem of woven words — what good is it,
to follow and fade with all else when east winds blow?

AFTER his period of exile, the poet was ordered to assume the post of governor of Teng-chou, a district on the north shore of the Shantung Peninsula. He arrived on the fifteenth day of the tenth lunar month of 1085, and five days later received orders to come to the capital to assume an even higher position. The mirage, which appeared off the coast in the Gulf of Pohai, was said to be an apparition of the palace of the Sea God, the abode of the immortals, and the poet bases his discussion of it on the description of such a palace in the poem entitled "Lord of the River," the eighth of the "Nine Songs" attributed to Ch'ü Yüan (fl. 300 B.C.), particularly the lines: "Of fish scales is his house, with dragon halls, / Gates of purple cowrie, palaces of pearl." (See the translator's *Early Chinese Literature,* pp. 244-45.)

Line 3. "Floating world." The earth was believed to float upon a vast cosmic sea.

Line 15. "Governor of Ch'ao-yang." The T'ang poet and statesman Han Yü, who was exiled to the south in 819. Su is here referring to a poem which Han Yü composed when he passed Mount Heng, one of the five sacred mountains of China, situated in southern Hunan. It is entitled "A Poem on Visiting the Shrine at Mount Heng," and in it Han Yü relates that, as it was autumn when he arrived at the foot of Mount Heng, the peaks were hidden in mist, but he offered up a prayer, and in response the peaks immediately became visible. This, he declares, is evidence that his honest heart has moved the spirits of the mountain. Su, following the wording of Han Yü's poem, refers to Mount Heng by the names of two of its peaks, Shih-lin and Chu-jung. But he is confused about the date and circumstances of Han Yü's poem. It was written in 805, when Han Yü was passing through the vicinity of Mount Heng on his way from Yang-shan to Chiang-ling-fu in Hupeh; not, as Su's wording implies, when he was on his way back from exile in Ch'ao-yang in 820.

When Yü-k'o Painted Bamboo (1087)

WRITTEN on paintings of bamboo by Wen Yü-k'o in Ch'ao Pu-chih's
collection: three poems.

89 When Yü-k'o painted bamboo,
    he saw bamboo only, never people.
    Did I say he saw no people?
    So rapt he forgot even himself —
    he himself became bamboo,
    putting out fresh growth endlessly.
    Chuang Tzu no longer with us,
    who can fathom this uncanny power?

WRITTEN when the poet was in the capital serving as a member of the Han-lin
Academy, which drafted government documents, and acting as tutor to the young
ruler, Emperor Che-tsung. Wen Yü-k'o or Wen T'ung (1018-79) was a cousin of the
poet's from Szechwan, a noted painter whose bamboos were especially famous. Ch'ao
Pu-chih (1053-1110) was one of the poet's leading disciples. This is the first poem of
the series.

Creek Crisscrosses the Meadow (1087)

WRITTEN to accompany Li Shih-nan's "Autumn Scene": two poems.

89 Creek crisscrosses the meadow, banks scarred where water rose;
in sparse woods, frost-burned roots stick out at a slant.
Little boat with a single oar – where's it going?
Home south of the river to a village of yellow leaves.

LI SHIH-NAN was a contemporary of the poet, particularly noted for his landscapes.
This is the first of the two poems.

Who Says a Painting Must Look Like Life? (1087)

WRITTEN on paintings of flowering branches by Secretary Wang of Yen-ling: two poems.

90   Who says a painting must look like life?
He sees only with children's eyes.
Who says a poem must stick to the theme?
Poetry is certainly lost on him.
Poetry and painting share a single goal –
clean freshness and effortless skill.
Pien Luan's sparrows live on paper;
Chao Ch'ang's flowers breathe with soul.
But what are they beside these scrolls,
bold sketches, with spirit in every stroke?
Who'd think one dot of red
could call up a whole unbounded spring!

THE FULL NAME and identity of Secretary Wang are unknown. This is the first of the two poems, probably written to accompany a picture of a branch of flowering plum, the symbol of early spring.

Above the River, Heavy on the Heart (1088)

WRITTEN on a painting entitled "Misty Yangtze and Folded Hills" in the collection of Wang Ting-kuo.

92 Above the river, heavy on the heart, thousand-fold hills:
layers of green floating in the sky like mist.
Mountains? clouds? too far away to tell
till clouds part, mist scatters, on mountains that remain.
Then I see, in gorge cliffs, black-green clefts
where a hundred waterfalls leap from the sky,
threading woods, tangling rocks, lost and seen again,
falling to valley mouths to feed swift streams.
Where the river broadens, mountains part, foothill forests end,
a small bridge, a country store set against the slope:
now and then travelers pass beyond tall trees;
a fishing boat – one speck where the river swallows the sky.
Tell me, where did you get this painting
sketched with these clean and certain strokes?
I didn't know the world had such places –
I'll go at once and buy some land!
Perhaps you've never seen those hidden spots
near Wu-ch'ang and Fan-k'ou, where I lived five years –
spring wind shook the river and sky was everywhere;
evening clouds rolled back the rain on gentle mountains;
from scarlet maples, crows flapped down to keep the boatman
     company;
from tall pines, snow tumbled, startling his drunken sleep.
The peach flowers, the stream are in the world of men!
Wu-ling is not for immortals only –
rivers, hills, clean and empty: I live in city dust,
and though roads go there, they're not for me.
I give back your picture and sigh three sighs;
my hill friends will soon be sending poems to call me home.

Line 18. "Wu-ch'ang and Fan-k'ou." Places south of the Yangtze opposite Huang-chou.

Line 23. "The stream." This is Su's answer to a poem by Li Po (701-62) entitled "Dialogue in the Mountains":

> You ask why I live in these jade-green mountains –
> I smile and do not answer – my mind is still.
> Peach flowers on the stream flow far away;
> This is another world, not that of men.

The peach flowers refer to the paradise which the poet T'ao Yüan-ming (also call T'ao Ch'ien) (365-427) described in his "Record of the Peach Flower Spring," an isolated valley inhabited by happy peasants and approached through a peach forest in Wu-ling, which a fisherman stumbled upon once but could never find again.

Presented to Liu Ching-wen (1090)

93   Lotuses have withered, they put up no umbrellas to the rain;
one branch of chrysanthemum holds out against frost.
Good sights of all the year I'd have you remember,
but especially now, with citrons yellow and tangerines still green.

Setting Off Early on the Huai River (1092)

94   Pale moon dipping in clouds, dawn bugle wailing;
      faint wind carves green scales on the water.
      Will I spend all my life on rivers and lakes?
      I count to myself — ten trips up and down the Huai.

A Pair of Rocks, with Introduction (1092)

WHEN I CAME to Yang-chou I acquired two rocks. One is green in color, like a long range of mountain peaks, with a cave in it extending all the way to the back of the rock. The other is pure white and can be used as a mirror. I filled a basin with water and set them in it near my desk. Then suddenly I recalled how one day when I was in Ying-chou I dreamed that a man came and asked me to head a certain government office, and the plaque on the office read "Ch'ou Lake." When I woke up, I recited to myself Tu Fu's lines:

> Ten thousand years old, the cave of Ch'ou Lake;
> its secret passage leads to a little heaven apart.[1]

So as a joke I wrote this little poem to give my fellow officials a laugh.

95 In dreams it seemed so real, now awake, it doesn't –
    drawing water, setting them in the basin, I feel foolish.
    Yet I see jade-white crests stretching to Mount T'ai-po;
    following the birds' path, I soar over O-mei.
    Autumn breezes come to make mist and clouds for me,
    the dawn sun floods my plants and trees.
    And that point of glimmery light – where does it come from?
    How this old man longs to go live in that Ch'ou Lake mountain!

---

1. The opening lines in the fourteenth poem in the series "Miscellaneous Poems on Ch'in-chou," written in 759. Ch'ou Lake is the name of a lake and mountain near Ch'in-chou in Kansu. Taoist lore speaks often of "heavens" or otherworldly realms that are hidden underground in certain mountains and can be reached only through narrow cave passages. The poet imagines that the tiny cave in his rock leads to such a realm.

Drinking Wine (1092)

FOLLOWING the rhymes of T'ao's "Drinking Wine." As far as quantity goes, I drink very little, but I always enjoy having a wine cup in my hand, and very often I drop off to sleep right where I'm sitting. People think I'm drunk, though in fact my head is perfectly clear – actually you couldn't say I'm either drunk or sober. Here in Yang-chou I drink as usual, though I always stop after noon. When my visitors for the day have left, I loosen my clothes, stretch out my feet, and sit where I am the rest of the day. I haven't had enough to drink to be really happy, and yet I feel an almost excessive exhilaration. So I decided to write some poems using the same rhymes as those used by T'ao Yüan-ming in his twenty poems entitled "Drinking Wine," in hopes that I could give some sort of expression to these nameless feelings. I am showing them to my brother Tzu-yu and to the scholar Ch'ao Pu-chih.

96 Master T'ao, I can't compete with you!
   Forever snarled up in official business,
   what can I do to break away,
   live just once a life like yours?
   Thorns grow in the field of the mind;
   clear them and there's no finer place.
   Free the mind – let it move with the world
   and doubt nothing it finds there!
   In wine I stumbled on unexpected joy.
   Now I always have an empty cup in hand.

97 I dreamed I was back in primary school,
   my hair tied in two knots like a boy
   (I'd forgotten that now it's gray),
   and I was reciting the *Analects*.
   The world at best is a children's game;
   like my dream – upside-down.
   Only in wine is man himself,

his mind a cave empty of doubt.
He can fall from a carriage and never get hurt –
Chuang Tzu told us no lies.
I call my son to fetch paper and brush
and take down drunken thoughts as they come.

CH'AO PU-CHIH was at this time serving as vice governor of Yang-chou. T'ao Yüan-ming's famous set of poems, written after he had quit official life in 405 and was living in retirement as a farmer, are philosophical meditations on the ills of the time and the pleasures of rural life. These are the first and twelfth of Su's series.

97, line 9. "Fall from a carriage" – a reference to *Chuang Tzu*, Sec. 19, *Ta-sheng* chapter: "When a drunken man falls from a carriage, though the carriage may be going very fast, he won't be killed…because his spirit is whole. He didn't know he was riding, and he doesn't know he has fallen out."

Long Ago I Lived in the Country (1093)

WRITTEN at the end of a painting on the "Restoration of the Herdsmen" by Ch'ao Yüeh-chih.

98 Long ago I lived in the country,
knew only sheep and cows.
Down smooth riverbeds on the cow's back,
steady as a hundred-weight barge,
a boat that needs no steering – while banks slipped by,
I stretched out and read a book – she didn't care.
Before us we drove a hundred sheep,
heeding my whip as soldiers heed a drum;
I didn't lay it on too often –
only stragglers I gave a lash to.
In lowlands, grass grows tall,
but tall grass is bad for cows and sheep;
so we headed for the hills, leaping sags and gullies
(climbing up and down made my muscles strong),
through long woods where mist wet my straw coat and hat....
But those days are gone – I see them only in a painting.
No one believes me when I say I regret
not staying a herdsman all my life.

WRITTEN after the poet had returned from Yang-chou to the capital. Ch'ao Yüeh-chih (1059-1129) was a cousin of Ch'ao Pu-chih and a student of the poet's. The painting represented the restoration of the system of employing government herdsmen to tend the royal flocks under King Hsüan of the Chou (r. 827-782 B.C.), a system that had been abandoned during the troubled times of his predecessor, King Li.

Part Five

SECOND EXILE: 1094 TO 1101

Held Up by Head Winds on the Tz'u-hu-chia: Five Poems (1094)

99   Stays and mast whine in the sky;
the boatman sleeps soundly by white-blossomed waves.
Mooring lines must know how I feel –
their weak strands hold fast against measureless wind.

100   Slimmer and slimmer – my chances of going home;
endless green hills ahead, water touching sky.
Even here a small boat comes selling cakes.
I'm glad to hear there's a village this side of the mountain.

IN THE PREVIOUS YEAR the poet had been assigned to the post of governor of Ting-chou in the far northeast, near Peking. This year an order came for his exile to the region of Canton; once more his enemies were in power at court. He left Ting-chou, visited his brother on the way, and had passed Nanking on the Yangtze when his boat was detained by adverse winds in the Tz'u-hu-chia, a tributary of the Yangtze. The first and second poems of the series.

Seven Thousand Miles Away (1094)

EIGHTH MONTH, seventh day. Entered the Kan River and passed Fearful Rapids.

101   Seven thousand miles away, a gray-haired man;
eighteen rapids, one little boat:
hills recall Hsi-huan – thoughts roam far away;
"fearful" they call this place – it makes me want to cry.
A long wind follows us, bellying the sail;
rain-fed current bears the boat through rippled shallows.
With my experience, they ought to make me official boatman –
I know more of rivers than merely where the ferries cross.

THE BOAT on which the poet was traveling had crossed Lake Poyang and entered the Kan River, noted for its eighteen stretches of rapids, of which Fearful Rapids was the first.

Line 3. "Hsi-huan." An abbreviation for Ts'o-hsi-huan or "False Joy," the name of a place on the mountain road out of Szechwan, the poet's birthplace. It was so called because travelers supposed when they reached there that the worst of the journey was over, though in fact there were many hard stretches still ahead.

Feet Stuck Out, Singing Wildly (1094)

GOVERNOR CHAN came to visit me, bringing wine. Using a previous rhyme of mine, he composed a poem, and I responded with another poem in the same rhyme.

102 Feet stuck out, singing wildly, I beat an old clay tub;
singeing fur, roasting meat, like a northwest nomad.
Outriders shout through the market – you've come to fetch me;
on Fishing Point, sand is swept, wine jars set out.
Boys from the foothills crowd to watch us dance;
white bones by the river remember your kindness.
One cloud, a slanting sun – I gaze southwest
and envy crows that know the way back home.

IN THE TENTH MONTH the poet arrived at Hui-chou on the Tung River, east of Canton, which had been designated as his place of exile, and was living in a Buddhist temple. Chan Fan, the governor of Hui-chou at the time, treated him with great kindness.

Line 6. "White bones." The region had suffered from local wars and many corpses had been left unburied. A note by the poet explains that Governor Chan ordered all the bones of such victims to be collected and given proper burial. The poet is probably hinting that, should he die in exile, he would hope the governor to show a similar kindness by arranging for his burial.

Days of Rain; the Rivers Have Overflowed: Two Poems (1095)

103   From Yüeh-ching hilltop clouds race down;
      along the Tsang-ko, water like sky.
      I move my bed here and there, dodging leaks in the roof;
      Tanka shift their houseboats from cove to cove.
      Dragons scoop up fish and shrimp, drop them with the rain;
      men follow dogs and chickens to sleep on top of walls.
      I'll mark the ground floor where water flooded the stairs
      so they'll recall my year here south of the mountains.

104   Drenching rain hisses down, cooling the evening;
      I lie and listen to banyan noise echo on the porch.
      By feeble lamp shine, I shake off a dream;
      curtains and blinds, half soaked, breathe old incense.
      High waves shake the bed, spray blows from the cistern;
      dark wind rocks the trees — they clink like jade.
      Even if it clears I have no place to go —
      let it keep on all night pelting the empty stairs.

WRITTEN at Hui-chou. The poet was living on the Tung or East River, which to the west flowed into the West River and the Tsang-ko to form the Pearl River, on which present day Canton is situated.

103, line 4. "Tanka." Aboriginal people who lived on houseboats on the rivers around Canton.

103, line 5. What the poet means by this line I don't know. Perhaps he is referring to some legend or local saying.

I'm a Frightened Monkey Who's Reached the Forest (1095)

TO THE SAME RHYMES as T'ao's "Going Back to the Country," six poems. On the 4th day of the 3rd month, I took a trip to the Grotto of Buddha's Footprint at White Water Mountain. I bathed at the hot spring there, dried my hair in the sun at the foot of the waterfall, and came home singing at the top of my voice. Returning by palanquin, I became absorbed in conversation with my companions and did not realize we had reached Lichee Nut Cove. The evening sun was pale and washed-out, the shadows of the bamboo deserted and lonely, and the lichee nuts hung in great clusters like water chestnuts. An old man of eighty-five who lived nearby pointed to the nuts and said, "When these are ready to eat, why don't you bring some wine and come visit me?" I was delighted at the idea and promised I would do so. I took a nap as soon as I got home, and woke up to hear my son Kuo chanting T'ao Yüan-ming's six poems on "Going Back to the Country." I decided to compose poems of my own using the same rhymes. When I was living in Yang-chou, I wrote twenty poems on the rhymes of T'ao's "Drinking Wine" series, and now I have written these. I intend to keep on until eventually I have composed poems to the rhymes of T'ao's complete works.

105   I'm a frightened monkey who's reached the forest,
a tired horse unharnessed at last,
my mind a void to fill with new thoughts;
surroundings are old to me — I see them in dreams.
River gulls flock around, growing tamer;
old Tanka men drop in to visit.
South pond lotus spreads green coins;
north hill bamboo sends up purple shoots.
Bring-the-jug (what does he know about wine?)
inspires me with a fine idea.

The spring river had a beautiful poem
but, drunk, I dropped it somewhere far away.

WRITTEN at Hui-chou. Kuo was Su's third son. He and the poet's concubine, Chao-yün, were the only members of his household who accompanied him in exile. (His first wife had died in 1065, his second wife in 1093; Chao-yün, who had been living with the poet since 1074, died in 1096.) Actually there are only five poems in T'ao Yüan-ming's "Going Back to the Country" series; Su's sixth poem follows the rhyme of a poem about T'ao Yüan-ming by Chiang Yen (444-505). This is the second poem in the series.

Line 9. "Bring-the-jug." The name of a bird, so called because its cry is said to resemble the words *t'i-hu* or "Bring the jug!"

Eating Lichees, Two Poems with Introduction (1096)

IN THE EAST HALL of the governor of Hui-chou there is a memorial shrine to the late prime minister, Lord Ch'en Wen-hui.[1] Beside the hall is a lichee tree that Lord Ch'en himself planted. This year it was loaded with fruit, and after the governor had eaten all he wanted, he handed out the rest to his clerks and underlings. Fruit that was too high up to reach he left for the monkeys to pick.

106   Here by Mount Lo-fu all four seasons are spring –
loquats, arbutus berries, one new taste after another.
Daily I devour lichees, three hundred at a time,
don't care how long I stay here south of the mountains!

THE SECOND of two poems.

---

1. Ch'en Yao-tso (963-1044), a high official who at one time served as substitute governor of Hui-chou.

White Crane Hill (1097)

AT MY NEW PLACE at White Crane Hill we dug a well forty feet deep. We struck a layer of rock partway down, but finally broke through and got to water.

107 Seacoast wears you out with damp and heat;
my new place is better – high and cool.
In return for the sweat of hiking up and down
I've a dry spot to sleep and sit.
But paths to the river are a rocky hell;
I wince at the water bearer's aching back.
I hired four men, put them to work
hacking through layers of obdurate rock.
Ten days and they'd gone only eight or ten feet;
below was a stratum of solid blue stone.
Drills all day struck futile sparks –
when would we ever see springs bubble up?
I'll keep you filled with rice and wine,
you keep your drills and hammers flying!
Mountain rock must end some time –
stubborn as I am, I won't give up.
This morning the houseboy told me with joy
they're into dirt soft enough to knead!
At dawn the pitcher brought up milky water;
by evening, it was clearer than an icy stream.
All my life has been like this –
what way to turn and not run into blocks?
But Heaven has sent me a dipper of water;
arm for a pillow, my happiness overflows.

IN THE PREVIOUS YEAR the poet had bought some unused land at a place called White Crane Hill overlooking the Tung River in Hui-chou, and had built a house, which he completed in the second month of this year.

Line 24. "Arm for a pillow." An allusion to *Analects* VII. 15: "The Master said, 'With coarse grain to eat, water to drink, and my bended arm for a pillow – I still have joy in the midst of these things. Riches and honor unrighteously acquired are to me as a floating cloud.'"

Three Delights in My Place of Exile (1097)

108   *Getting Up in the Morning and Combing My Hair*

Sound sleep, sea of inner breath stirring;
boundless, it ascends to the cerebral palace.
The sun comes up, dew not yet dried,
dense mist shrouding the frosty pines.
This old comb's been with me so long —
teeth missing, still it makes fresh breezes.
With a single washing, ears and eyes brighten;
popping open, ten thousand pores come alive.
Young days, how I loved my sleep, loathed getting up —
dawn audiences at court were always a scramble,
no time even to give my head a good scratching,
and then the bother of putting on a hat! —
no different from a draft horse in the shafts,
wind-tousled mane full of dirt and sand.
Mounting my fancy saddle, jeweled bit jangling,
in truth it was like donning chains and shackles,
no telling when I'd be free again, unchained,
not even an old willow to rub my itches on! —
But who can describe the delight I know now?
I'll send copies to the gentlemen with gold seals at their waist.

THE FIRST of three poems. The other two are entitled "By the Afternoon Window, Sitting and Dozing," and "Before Going to Bed, Soaking My Feet." The poet was suffering from swollen feet, probably due to beriberi, and soaked his feet to relieve the swelling.

Lines 1–2. The poet employs Taoist terminology to describe the physical sensation of a good night's rest.

Line 20. "Gentlemen with gold seals at their waist" are the high government officials who sent the poet into exile. It is said that one of them ordered Su to move from Hui-Chou to Tan-chou because rumor reached him that Su was actually enjoying himself in Hui-chou. As these poems illustrate, Su remained defiantly determined to continue enjoying his life in exile.

Half-sober, Half-drunk (1098)

HAVING DRUNK some wine, I went out alone for a walk and visited the house of four Li families, Tzu-yün, Wei, Hui, and Hsien-chüeh.

109   Half-sober, half-drunk, I call on the Lis;
       bamboo spikes, rattan creepers tangle every step.
       Following cow turds I find my way back —
       home beyond the cattle pen, west and west again.

THE YEAR BEFORE, the poet had been ordered to leave Hui-chou, where he had just settled down in his new house, and proceed to Tan-chou on the west side of Hainan Island in the South China Sea. He could not have been sent farther away without being forced to leave China altogether. The Li or Loi people were non-Chinese aborigines of Hainan, though these friends of the poet apparently lived in or near the Chinese community.

Letting the Writing Brush Go Where It Will, Three Poems (1099)

I.

110 Old men scramble to get a look at my pointy black headcloth,
doubtless because it's proof I once held a government post.
On the old river road, where it branches three ways,
I stand alone in slanting sunlight, while others now and then go by.

II.

111 Boats from up north don't arrive – rice costs as much as pearls!
Getting drunk, eating my fill – not for half a dreary month.
But tomorrow the family to the east will sacrifice to the Kitchen
    God;
surely they'll send me over a chicken and a measure of wine.

THE SECOND and third poem in the series. The year-end sacrifice to the Kitchen God was carried out on the 23rd of the twelfth month by officials and on the following day by ordinary citizens.

Dipping Water from the River and Simmering Tea (1100)

112   Living water needs living fire to boil;
      lean over Fishing Rock, dip the clear deep current;
      store the spring moon in a big gourd, return it to the jar;
      divide the night stream with a little dipper, drain it into the kettle.
      Frothy water, simmering, whirls bits of tea;
      pour it and hear the sound of wind in pines.
      Hard to refuse three cups to a dried-up belly;
      I sit and listen – from the old town, the striking of the hour.

Black Muzzle (1100)

WHEN I CAME to Tan-chou, I acquired a watchdog named Black Muzzle. He was very fierce, but soon got used to people. He went with me to Ho-p'u, and when we passed Ch'eng-mai, he startled everyone on the road by swimming across the river. So as a joke I wrote this poem for him.

113   Black Muzzle, south sea dog,
how lucky I am to be your master!
On scraps growing plump as a gourd,
never grumbling for fancier food.
Gentle by day, you learn to tell my friends;
ferocious by night, you guard the gate.
When I told you I was going back north,
you wagged your tail and danced with delight,
bounced along after the boy,
tongue out, dripping a shower of sweat.
You wouldn't go by the long bridge
but took a short cut across the clear deep bay,
bobbing along like a water bird,
scrambling up the bank fiercer than a tiger.
You steal meat — a fault, though a minor one,
but I'll spare you the whip this time.
You nod your head by way of thanks,
Heaven having given you no words.
Someday I'll get you to take a letter home —
Yellow Ears was your ancestor, I'm sure.

THIS YEAR the poet was ordered to leave Tan-chou and go to Ho-p'u in Lien-chou on the mainland opposite Hainan, the first sign that the worst of his exile was over. Ch'eng-mai is on the north coast of Hainan, near where the poet took the boat to the mainland.

Line 20. "Yellow Ears." Pet dog of the poet Lu Chi (261–303). When Lu Chi was in the capital at Loyang, he became worried because he had no news from his family in Wu, near the mouth of the Yangtze. So he wrote a letter and, putting it in a bamboo container, tied it to Yellow Ears' neck and sent it home by way of the dog.

I Thought I'd End My Days in a Hainan Village (1100)

WRITTEN at Tide-flow Hall at Ch'eng-mai Stop: two poems.

114 I thought I'd end my days in a Hainan village
but God sent Wu-yang to call back my soul.
Far, far, where sky lowers and eagles pass from sight:
a hairbreadth of green hill – the mainland there!

WRITTEN when the poet was about to take the boat for the mainland. This is the second of the two poems.

Line 2. "Wu-yang." A reference to the "Summons to the Soul," a poem attributed to Sung Yü (3rd cent. B.C.), in which God orders the sorceress Wu-yang to discover where the soul of Sung Yü's teacher, the exiled poet Ch'ü Yüan, has fled and summon it home again. By God, of course, Su means Emperor Hui-tsung, who ascended the throne this year and was recalling him from exile.

By the River at T'eng-chou, Getting Up at Night and Looking at the Moon, to Send to the Monk Shao (1100)

115   River moon to light my mind,
      river water to wash my liver clean,
      moon like an inch-round pearl
      fallen into this white jade cup.
      My mind too is like this:
      a moon that's full, a river with no waves.
      Who is it gets up to dance?
      Let's hope there are more than three of you!
      In this pestilent land south of the mountains,
      still we have the cool river moonlight,
      and I know that in all heaven and earth
      there's no one not calm and at peace.
      By the bedside I have milky wine;
      the jar brims over as though full of white dew.
      I get drunk alone, sober up alone,
      the night air boundlessly fresh.
      I'll send word to the monk Shao,
      have him bring his zither and play under the moon,
      and then we'll board a little boat
      and in the night go down the Ts'ang-wu rapids.

THE POET, on his way home to the north, was about to leave T'eng-chou in Kwangsi and travel down the Ts'ang-wu River.

Lines 7-8. An allusion to Li Po's famous poem, "Drinking Alone Under the Moon," in which he speaks of three companions, the moon, his shadow, and himself, drinking and dancing together.

Bell and Drum on the South River Bank (1101)

FOLLOWING the rhymes of Chiang Hui-shu: two poems.

116 Bell and drum on the south river bank:
home! I wake startled from a dream.
Drifting clouds — so the world shifts;
lone moon — such is the light of my mind.
Rain drenches down as from a tilted basin;
poems flow out like water spilled.
The two rivers vie to send me off;
beyond treetops I see the slant of a bridge.

WRITTEN in the summer. The poet had traveled north, then east down the Yangtze to Chinkiang, and was now about to enter the Grand Canal to go south to Ch'ang-chou, where he planned to live the remainder of his life. He died on the 18th day of the seventh month of this year, shortly after reaching Ch'ang-chou. This is the second of the two poems.

About the translator

BURTON WATSON is among the most revered translators of classical Chinese and Japanese poetry. Born in 1925 in New Rochelle, N.Y., he served three years in the navy during World War II, before beginning Chinese studies at Columbia College. Among his dozens of translations of major works of Japanese and Chinese history, poetry, and philosophy, his *Chuang Tzu* is an acknowledged classic. He has edited *The Columbia Book of Chinese Poetry*, translated the *Lotus Sutra*, and received both the Gold Medal Award of the Translation Center at Columbia University and the PEN Translation Prize. Formerly Professor of Chinese at Columbia University, he now lives in Niigata, Japan, and devotes full time to translation.

Book design and composition by John D. Berry, using Aldus PageMaker 5.0 on an Apple Macintosh. The type is Monotype Bembo, a digitized version of the modern revival of a typeface originally cut by Francesco Griffo for the Venetian publisher Aldus Manutius, and used to print Cardinal Bembo's *De Ætna* in 1495. Printed on 55# Glatfelter Supple Opaque Recycled paper and bound by Thomson-Shore, Inc.